Water Resources Management

A World Bank Policy Paper

The World Bank
Washington, D.C.

© 1993 International Bank for Reconstruction
and Development / THE WORLD BANK
1818 H Street, N.W.
Washington, D.C. 20433 U.S.A.

Cover design by Walton Rosenquist and Beni Chibber-Rao

Library of Congress Cataloging-in-Publication Data
Water resources management.
      p.   cm. — (A World Bank policy paper)
   Includes bibliographical references.
   ISBN 0-8213-2636-8
   1. Water resources development—Developing countries.
   I. International Bank for Reconstruction and Development.
   II. Series.
   HD1702.W382   1993
   333.91′009172′6—dc20   93-31793
                                                                  CIP

ISBN 0-8213-2636-8
ISSN 1014-8124

Contents

Boxes

Tables

Glossary

Aquifer
: An underground stratum that is saturated with water and transmits water readily

Command and control
: A system of water management based on administrative allocations

Comprehensive framework
: An analytic framework for water resources that views water as a single resource with many uses and interlinkages with the ecological and socioeconomic system

Cost recovery
: Fee structures that cover the cost of providing the service

Decentralization
: The distribution of responsibilities for decisionmaking and operations to lower levels of government, community organizations, the private sector, and nongovernmental organizations

Demand management
: The use of price, quantitative restrictions, and other devices to limit the demand for water

Drip irrigation
: A localized drop-by-drop application of water that uses pipes, tubes, filters, emitters, and ancillary devices to deliver water to specific sites at a point or grid on the soil surface

Ecosystem	A complex system formed by the interaction of a community of organisms with its environment
Externality	The unintended real (nonmonetary) side effect of one party's actions on another party that is ignored in decisions made by the party causing the effects
Financial autonomy	The ability of an entity to operate and sustain its activities for a long period based on the revenue it collects from the users of its services
Gravity irrigation	A system that depends on sloping canals and fields to transport water to an irrigated site
Market failure	A divergence between the market outcome (without intervention) and the economically efficient solution
Opportunity cost	The value of goods or services forgone, including environmental goods and services, when a scarce resource is used for one purpose instead of for its next best alternative use
Riparian state	A state through or along which a portion of a river flows or a lake lies
River basin	A geographical area determined by the watershed limits of a system of water, including surface and underground water, flowing into a common terminus
Sewage	Liquid refuse or waste matter carried off by sewers
Sewerage	The removal and disposal of sewage and surface water by sewer systems
Tubewells	Circular wells consisting of tubes or pipes placed in holes bored into the ground to tap groundwater supplies from one or more aquifers

Unaccounted-for water	The difference between the volume of water delivered to a supply system and the volume of water accounted for by legitimate consumption, whether metered or not (or the measured volume of supplied water that is produced or treated less the water that is consumed legitimately, the difference being what is stolen or lost)
Watercourse	A system of surface and underground waters that constitute, by virtue of their physical relationship, a unitary whole and flow into a common terminus
Watershed	An area drained by a river or stream system
Watershed management	A process of formulating and implementing a course of action that involves a region's natural and human resources taking into account social, political, economic, environmental, and institutional factors operating within the watershed, the surrounding river basin, and other relevant regions to achieve desired social objectives
Wetlands	Areas of marsh, fen, peat land, or water that include natural, artificial, permanent, and temporary areas with static or flowing water that is fresh, brackish, or marine

Acknowledgments

This report was prepared by K. William Easter, Gershon Feder, Guy Le Moigne and Alfred M. Duda. Significant contributions were also made by Randolph Anderson, Jeremy Berkoff, Ramesh Bhatia, Hans Binswanger, John Briscoe, Harold Frederiksen, John Hayward, Robert Hearne, Ulrich Kuffner, Pierre Landell-Mills, Geoffrey Matthews, Mohan Munasinghe, Francois-Marie Patorni, Michel Petit, Herve Plusquellec, William Price, Joanne Salop, Charles Sheerin, Ashok Subramanian, Bocar Thiam, Hans Wolter, and Mei Xie. The paper also benefited from consultations with colleagues from within and outside the Bank who are simply too numerous to list. Drafts of the paper were produced by Magdalene Z. Wu. Elizabeth Forsyth edited the paper, and Virginia Hitchcock coordinated publication.

Executive Summary

Water resources have been one of the most important areas of World Bank lending during the past three decades. Through its support for sector work and investments in irrigation, water supply, sanitation, flood control, and hydropower, the Bank has contributed to the development of many countries and helped provide essential services to many communities. Yet, as pointed out in reports of the Operations Evaluations Department, the investments supported by the Bank in the areas have often encountered implementation, operational, and social problems. Underlying these problems is a vicious cycle of poor-quality and unreliable services that result in consumers' unwillingness to pay, which, in turn, generates inadequate operating funds and a further deterioration in services. Moreover, the Bank and governments have not taken sufficient account of environmental concerns in the management of water resources.

The difficulties encountered by Bank-supported projects reflect a larger set of problems faced in water resource management, which are highlighted in the *World Development Report 1992: Development and the Environment* (1992d). Water is an increasingly scarce resource requiring careful economic and environmental management. The situation is exacerbated by rapid population growth and urbanization in developing countries. As the demand for water for human and industrial use has escalated, so has the competition for water used for irrigated agriculture. At the same time, the engineering and environmental costs are much higher for new water supplies than for sources already tapped. New challenges call for a new approach. Governments have often misallocated and wasted water, as well as permitted damage to the environment, as a result of institutional weaknesses, market failures, distorted policies, and misguided investments. Three problems in particular need to be addressed:

- Fragmented public investment programming and sector management, that have failed to take account of the interdependencies among agencies, jurisdictions, and sectors
- Excessive reliance on overextended government agencies that have neglected the need for economic pricing, financial accountability, and user participation and have not provided services effectively to the poor
- Public investments and regulations that have neglected water quality, health, and environmental concerns.

To manage water resources more effectively, a balanced set of policies and institutional reforms should be sought that will both harness the efficiency of market forces and strengthen the **capacity** of governments to carry out their essential roles.

A Framework for Improving Water Resource Management

The proposed new approach to managing water resources builds on the lessons of experience. At its core is the adoption of a comprehensive policy framework and the treatment of water as an economic good, combined with decentralized management and delivery structures, greater reliance on pricing, and fuller participation by stakeholders. The proposed approach is consistent with the Dublin Statement (1992) from the International Conference on Water and the Environment as well as with Agenda 21 from the 1992 United Nations Conference on Environment and Development.

Need for a comprehensive framework

The adoption of a comprehensive framework for analyzing policies and options would help guide decisions about managing water resources in countries where significant problems exist, or are emerging, concerning the scarcity of water, the efficiency of service, the allocation of water, or environmental damage. The complexity of the analysis would vary according to the country's capacity and circumstances, but relatively simple frameworks can often clarify priority issues. The framework would facilitate the consideration of relationships between the ecosystem and socioeconomic activities in river basins. The analysis should take account of social, environmental, and economic objectives; evaluate the status of water resources within each basin; and assess the level and composition of projected demand. Special attention should be given to the views of all stakeholders.

The results of the analyses at a river basin level would become part of the national strategy for water resource management. The analytical framework would provide the underpinnings for formulating public policies on regulations, incentives, public investment plans, and environmental protection and on the interlinkages among them. It would establish the parameters, ground rules, and price signals for decentralized implementation by government agencies and the private sector. Decentralizing the delivery of water services and adopting pricing that induces efficient use of water are key elements of sound water resource management. But, for decentralized management to be effective, a supportive legal framework and adequate regulatory capacity are required, as well as a system of water charges to endow water entities with operational and financial autonomy for efficient and sustainable delivery of services.

Country focus of the policy

The comprehensive analytical framework outlined above will need to be tailored to the situations and constraints facing individual countries. Many of the countries with limited renewable water resources are in the Middle East, North Africa, Central Asia, and Sub-Saharan Africa, where populations are growing fastest. Elsewhere, water scarcity may be less of a problem at the national level but is nevertheless severe in many areas such as in northern China, western and southern India, western South America, and large parts of Pakistan and Mexico. For some countries, such as those in Eastern Europe, pollution is the largest problem affecting water resources. In much of Africa, implementation capacity is a critical issue exacerbated by the frequency of prolonged droughts. In some countries, water resource management is not yet a significant problem. These differences among regions and countries will shape the design of strategies and programs for a given country.

Water policy objectives

Differences among countries notwithstanding, water resource management that follows the principles of comprehensive analysis, opportunity cost pricing, decentralization, stakeholder participation, and environmental protection outlined in this volume will yield more coherent policies and investments across sectors, promote conservation, and improve the efficiency of water allocation. The objective is to achieve, over time, the following improvements:

- *For industry,* extensive water conservation and protection of groundwater sources. Experience in industrial countries suggests that controlling pollution will also substantially reduce the quantity of water used per unit of industrial output.
- *For water supply and sanitation,* more efficient and accessible delivery of water services and sewage collection, treatment, and disposal, with the ultimate goal of providing universal coverage. This will be achieved by extending existing supplies through water conservation and reuse and by using other sustainable methods. Greater involvement of the private sector, nongovernmental organizations, and user groups will be required, as will cost recovery to ensure financial viability while applying graduated fees to assist the poor.
- *For irrigation and hydropower,* modernized irrigation practices, greater attention to cost recovery, drainage and salinity control, measures to reduce pollution from agricultural activities, improvements in operation and maintenance of existing systems, and investments in small-scale irrigation and various water-harvesting methods. This calls for the development of institutions and technologies that respond to the needs of farmers for higher-quality services, including greater participation of community groups and user associations, while reinforcing the efficient management of demand. Particular attention will be given to the needs of small-scale farmers, who comprise most of the agricultural community. Greater priority should be given to managing the demand for energy, identifying small-scale and renewable energy alternatives, promoting watershed conservation practices, and retrofitting and enhancing dam facilities.
- *For the environment and poverty alleviation,* more rigorous attention to minimizing resettlement, maintaining biodiversity, and protecting ecosystems in the design and implementation of water projects. Water and energy supplies gained through conservation and improved efficiency can be used instead of developing new supplies to extend service to the poor and maintain water-dependent ecosystems. Low-cost and environmentally benign methods of developing new water supplies for agriculture, rural drinking water, and industry will be pursued. The water supply needs of rivers, wetlands, and fisheries will be considered in decisions concerning the operation of reservoirs and the allocation of water.

The World Bank Policy

The Bank's overarching objective is to reduce poverty by supporting the efforts of countries to promote equitable, efficient, and sustainable development. This entails support for the provision of potable water and sanitation facilities, flood control, and water for productive activities in an economically viable, environmentally sustainable, and socially equitable manner. The new approach is designed to help countries achieve these objectives more effectively while sustaining the water environment, and the Bank will support member governments to that end. The Bank will give priority to countries where water is scarce or where the problems of water allocation, service efficiency, or environmental degradation are serious. In these countries, through its economic and sector work, lending, and participation in international initiatives, the Bank will promote policy reforms, institutional adaptation and capacity building, environmental protection and restoration, and, when requested, cooperation in the management of international watercourses. Because of the crucial interdependencies between water and other sectors, the Bank will incorporate water resource policy and management issues in its country policy dialogues and in the formulation of country assistance strategies where water issues are considered to be significant.

A comprehensive analytical framework

The Bank will encourage and, when requested, selectively help countries develop a systematic analytical framework for managing water resources that is suitable for a country's needs, resources, and capacities. The framework will be designed so that options for public water management can be evaluated and compared in the context of a national water strategy that incorporates the interdependencies between water and land use. It will enable coherent, consistent policies and regulations to be adopted across sectors. To facilitate the introduction of such a framework, the Bank is ready to support capacity building through training, demonstrating participatory techniques, and helping in water resource assessments. The Bank will also promote the creation, enhancement, and use of hydrologic, hydrogeologic, socioeconomic, water quality, and environmental data bases for both groundwater and surface water, as well as help governments effectively use this information in decisionmaking.

Institutional and regulatory systems

The reform of water resource management policies will have implications for the institutions dealing with water resources. The Bank will assist governments in establishing a strong legal and regulatory framework for dealing with the pricing, monopoly organizations, environmental protection, and other aspects of water management. Similarly, the Bank will support the adaptation of institutional structures at the national and regional levels to coordinate the formulation and implementation of policies for improved water management, public investment programs, and drought planning. In many countries, institutional reform will focus on river basins as the appropriate unit for analysis and coordinated management. Such coordinating arrangements are particularly important in countries with federal structures, in which provincial or state governments have primary authority over the management of water resources in their jurisdictions. In such countries, before committing funds to support operations that have important interstate effects, the Bank will require legislation or other appropriate arrangements to establish effective coordination and agreed procedures for allocating water. The Bank will also use water resources sector loans to coordinate water resource activities across sectors.

Incentives

Many of the problems encountered in providing water services are due to the lack of incentives both for performance by providers and for efficiency by users. A key component of the reforms to be supported by the Bank will thus be greater reliance on incentives for efficiency and financial discipline. The Bank will highlight the importance of pricing and financial accountability by using estimated opportunity costs as a guide in setting water charges. In practice, immediate adoption of opportunity cost pricing may be politically difficult. Thus, given the low level of current cost recovery and the importance of finances in the sustainability of operations, pricing to ensure financial autonomy will be a good starting point.

Water-conserving technology

An important element in any strategy to conserve water will be incentives for adopting technologies and management approaches that increase the efficient use, allocation, and distribution of water. Such technologies and management approaches will make it easier to conserve water, to increase the efficiency of water use and conveyance, and to reuse wastewater. As water scarcity and waste disposal problems become more acute, adopting and improving water conservation practices, wastewater reuse systems, and overall approaches to reduce pollution will become increasingly important.

Poverty alleviation

Inadequate water services have a particularly adverse impact on the poor, facilitating the spread of disease, especially in crowded low-income areas. Thus, special efforts will be directed to meeting the water needs of the poor. Moreover, the health benefits of better hygiene and clean water should be emphasized so that the advantages of having an improved water supply can be fully realized. Where public finance is scarce, significant additional resources can often be mobilized within local communities. Efforts should be made to determine the level of services actually wanted by the poor. Research and experience suggest that the poor are willing to pay for reliable service. Indeed, in the face of unreliable service, the poor often pay more for less water, which they typically receive from street vendors. Water entities that have a financial stake in serving the poor are more likely to provide them with better, more sustainable services. "Social fees," whereby the better-off cross-subsidize the poor, as well as budgetary transfers to subsidize connections can be used. However, caution is required. Assigning noncommercial objectives to a public enterprise may undermine the achievement of its service objectives, possibly initiating a new round of the vicious cycle of unsatisfactory service and low collections. Policies that affect or change water rights should be carefully evaluated to ensure that they do not harm the poor, since water rights are often crucial for generating income. Where necessary, adjustments should be accompanied by compensatory measures.

Decentralization

Because of their limited financial and administrative resources, governments need to be selective in the responsibilities they assume for water resources. The principle is that nothing should be done at a higher level of government that can be done satisfactorily at a lower level. Thus, where local or private capabilities exist and where an appropriate regulatory system can be established, the Bank will support central government efforts to decentralize responsibilities to local governments and to transfer service delivery functions to the private sector, to financially autonomous public corporations, and to community organizations such as water user associations. The privatization of public water service agencies, or their transformation into financially autonomous entities, and the use of management contracts for service delivery will be encouraged. Arrangements for ensuring performance accountability and for putting in place an appropriate regulatory framework to set and enforce environmental protection standards and to prevent inefficient monopoly pricing will be incorporated into Bank-supported activities. These steps should improve incentives for cost recovery and service provision and give users a sense of ownership and participation. In countries where provincial or municipal capabilities are inadequate to manage a complex system of water resources, the Bank will support training and capacity building to improve local management so that decentralization can eventually be achieved.

Participation

Participation is a process in which stakeholders influence policy formulation, alternative designs, investment choices, and management decisions affecting their communities and establish the necessary sense of ownership. As communities increase their participation in managing water resources, project selection, service delivery, and cost recovery will likely improve. Therefore, the Bank will encourage the participation of beneficiaries and affected parties in planning, designing, implementing, and managing the projects it supports. In environmental assessments, the Bank requires consultation with affected people and local nongovernmental organizations, and will additionally promote the participation of concerned people—including the poor, indigenous people, and disadvantaged groups—in the water-related operations it supports. Special attention will be given to the participation of women because they are essentially the managers of domestic water. The Bank will encourage governments to follow these principles more broadly in their investment programs and other activities related to water resources.

Environmental protection

Preservation of the environment and the resource base are essential for sustainable development. The protection, enhancement, and restoration of water quality and the abatement of water pollution will therefore be a focus of Bank-supported operations, particularly since providing safe drinking water is so critical to maintaining and improving human health. Accordingly, the Bank will increase its support of government efforts to improve and expand sanitation and the collection and treatment of wastewater. Similarly, the Bank will promote the use of efficiency pricing and "the-polluter-pays" principle through the imposition of pollution charges to encourage water conservation and reduce pollution. For industrial waste, mining runoff, and wastewater discharges, a balanced strategy involving economic incentives, effective legislation and regulatory systems, and guidelines for levels of pollution control will be used to reduce effluents at the source—especially toxic substances—and to stimulate reuse. For pollution originating from agricultural activities, the Bank will support initiatives that restore and protect surface and subsurface waters degraded by agricultural pollutants and that minimize soil erosion. The Bank will assist governments in developing strategies and cost-effective mechanisms for the ecologically sustainable management, protection, and restoration of recharge areas and water-dependent ecosystems, such as wetlands, riverine floodplain areas, estuaries, and coastal zones. Investments that involve resettlement should be avoided or minimized, and, where resettlement is necessary, former incomes and living standards should be restored or improved. Given the increasing importance of groundwater, especially in arid and semiarid areas, the Bank will pay attention to the linkages between ground and surface water in managing river basins and will support the establishment of government programs and policies, including land use policies, that restore and protect the quality of groundwater and preserve groundwater recharge areas.

Upgrading skills

In tandem with the promotion of a comprehensive framework and with institutional and policy reforms, country policy analysts, planners, managers, and technicians will need to upgrade their skills. Accordingly, where water resource management issues are significant, the Bank will support the training needed to deal with cross-sectoral analysis; with legal, regulatory, and privatization issues; and with river basin management, flood and drought planning, environmental protection, project formulation and evaluation, demand forecasting, and participatory management. The Economic Development Institute of the World Bank will be an important element in this training effort, through a special initiative to support the implementation of the new policy.

Designing country programs

Countries differ in their water requirements and endowments, their poverty profiles, their institutional capacities, and the problems they face from environmental degradation. Thus, the design of relevant reforms, and the time frame for implementation, will need to be developed and evaluated case by case. Nonetheless, introducing the recommended reforms will typically entail difficult political choices, and commitments by governments will therefore be essential. Given the present status of water resource management and institutions in many countries, implementing the necessary changes will take time. Accordingly,

- In countries with significant water management problems, the Bank will, in collaboration with other international and national agencies, assist governments through sector work, technical assistance, and environmental action plans in identifying and formulating priority policy and institutional reforms and investments and in determining their appropriate sequencing. These priorities—and the degree of government commitment to them—will be highlighted in the country assistance strategy and will guide the sectoral lending program.
- The priority reforms and activities to be addressed in analytic work and referred to in the country assistance strategy will deal with issues such as the appropriate (a) incentive framework and pricing, (b) service delivery to the poor, (c) public investment priorities, (d) environmental restoration and protection, (e) water resource assessment and data requirements, (f) comprehensive analytical framework, and (g) legislation, institutional structures, and capacities. Assessing the degree of government commitment to implementing the requisite reforms will be an important part of the analysis.
- Progress in implementing the identified priorities will be monitored through normal Bank interactions with the country. When inadequate progress on priority actions is judged to cause serious misuse of resources and to hamper the viability of water-related investments, Bank lending in this area will be limited to providing potable water to poor households and to operations designed to conserve water and protect its quality without additionally drawing on a country's water resources. Such operations include sanitation, waste treatment, water reuse and recycling, abatement of water pollution, drainage, and rehabilitation of the distribution systems. These investments will be assessed on their individual merits.
- Individual water lending operations should discuss the linkage to priorities for reform, investment, and Bank support as well as the likely impact of the overall water-related program. The analysis of operations will include an assessment of the implications for other water-using subsectors within the relevant regional setting, most likely a river basin. Relevant pricing issues, cost recovery, and financial autonomy and sustainability will receive particular attention. The rationale for institutional arrangements for implementation, particularly the division of responsibilities between

government and nongovernmental or financially autonomous entities, will be provided. The Bank requires the assessment of the environmental impact of projects, as well as environmental assessments of the entire river system for significant water-related projects, and full consultation with affected people and local organizations.

International watercourses

Existing guidelines describe Bank policy on the financing of projects dealing with international waterways. The Bank, together with other international organizations, will help countries improve the management of shared international water resources by, for example, supporting the analysis of development opportunities forgone because of international water disputes. Through technical, financial, and legal assistance, the Bank, if requested, will help governments establish or strengthen institutions, such as river basin organizations, to address transnational water management activities. Furthermore, the Bank will support studies and consultations to review available organizational arrangements and help countries develop alternative solutions. In initial contacts with riparians, the Bank will avoid setting preconditions, exploring instead the most appropriate form of assistance. The Bank will be sensitive at all times to the interests of other riparian parties, since all parties must be treated in an even-handed manner. The focus will be on international watercourses in which the Bank's assistance is likely to have a substantial effect. In addition, the incremental cost of actions taken by riparian states to protect international water resources and river basins will continue to be financed within the framework of the Global Environment Facility. The Bank will promote the acquisition of knowledge concerning internationally shared groundwater to provide a basis for establishing guidelines governing the Bank's activities in this area.

Implementation

To help implement its water resource management policy, the Bank will undertake a range of activities, including the preparation of guidelines and best-practices papers, staff and country training programs, capacity building, and the development of coordination mechanisms to improve the management of water resources. More specifically, in collaboration with the United Nations Development Programme, a guide on capacity building is being prepared for countries interested in formulating strategies for managing water resources. Guides are also being prepared on establishing water resource information systems, on best practices for setting up coordinating mechanisms, on generalized economic models for river basin analysis, and on best-management practices for water user associations. Regional units are preparing regional water strategies, which incorporate the recommendations of this water policy within the specific circumstances of their areas. The skill mix of available and required Bank staff in the area of water resource management has been analyzed, and training programs, workshops, and seminars are being prepared to upgrade existing staff skills. Pilot projects will be used to implement some of the newer aspects of the water policy such as decentralization and opportunity cost pricing. Finally, the implementation of the new water policy will be reviewed in two years.

1

Introduction

Water resources have been one of the most important areas of World Bank lending during the past three decades. Through its support for investments in irrigation, water supply, sanitation, flood control, and hydropower, the Bank has contributed to the development of many countries and helped provide essential services to many communities. Yet, as pointed out in studies of the Operations Evaluation Department, the investments supported by the Bank in these areas have often been hampered by implementation and by operational, environmental, and social problems. These difficulties are symptomatic of the larger set of problems faced in managing water resources, which are highlighted in the *World Development Report 1992: Development and the Environment* (World Bank 1992d). A new approach, recognizing that water is a scarce natural resource—subject to many interdependencies in conveyance and use—should be adopted by the Bank and its member countries. This volume articulates the key elements of such an approach and provides a framework for the Bank's water resource activities.

Water Problems and Bank Policy Objectives

The Bank's overarching objective is to reduce poverty by supporting the efforts of countries to promote equitable, efficient, and sustainable development. This entails support for the provision, in an economically viable, environmentally sustainable, and socially equitable manner, of potable water and sanitation facilities, protection from floods, and drainage as well as of water for productive activities. The new approach is designed to achieve these objectives more effectively while sustaining the water environment. Recognizing that water management has frequently been fragmented in the past, it stresses a comprehensive frame-

21

Box 1-1. United Nations Organizations and Water Resource Management

The Bank collaborates closely with many United Nations organizations involved in water resource management, including the United Nations Development Programme (UNDP), Food and Agricultural Organization (FAO), World Health Organization (WHO), United Nations International Children's Fund (UNICEF), World Meteorological Organization/United Nations Educational, Scientific, and Cultural Organization (WMO/UNESCO), United Nations Department of Economic and Social Development (UN-DESD), and United Nations Environment Programme (UNEP). These organizations also engage in collaborative programs among themselves.

The UNDP has supported major initiatives in the field of water resource management and collaborates with the Bank in both the irrigation and the water supply and sanitation subsectors at the country and global levels. It raises general public awareness through sponsorship and participation in major global conferences on water resources. Recently, it joined the Bank in preparing a program to help countries initiate comprehensive policies for managing water resources.

The FAO recently launched an International Action Program on Water and Sustainable Agricultural Development. The program highlights priority areas for action in agriculture in the context of sustainable agricultural development with special reference to water use.

The WHO works in collaboration with governments and international organizations to improve water quality and reduce the incidence of water-borne diseases. Its program for promoting environmental health provides technical support for community water supply and sanitation. In addition, it is engaged in an important effort to encourage safety in chemical use that will help protect supplies of fresh water from contamination.

UNICEF is involved in providing water to rural communities throughout the world and has been a partner of governments, the Bank, and other agencies in pioneering low-cost water supply technologies such as the Mark II hand pump and in developing institutional innovations with wider community participation.

UNESCO and the WMO actively sponsor the International Hydrological Program and recently, through their report on water resources assessment, stressed the importance of hydrological assessment as a first step in planning the use of water resources.

The UN-DESD, through its Science, Technology, Energy, Environment, and Natural Resources Division, helps countries to formulate policies and projects in water resources, including rural water supply, river basin development, and pollution control. It hosts the Intersecretariat Group for Water Resources.

The UNEP, through its own programs and through its support for the Global Environment Fund, brings a specialist's focus on environmental aspects and water quality to water resource management.

work for formulating country policies and public decisions that takes into account the interdependencies that characterize water resources. Observing the waste and inefficiencies that have resulted from the frequent failure to use prices and other instruments to manage demand and guide allocation, the new approach stresses the importance of using decentralized implementation processes and market forces to provide water services. Realizing that water use in all its forms impinges on natural ecosystems and the health of people, the new approach stresses the importance of assessing and mitigating the environmental consequences of public investments and of establishing effective regulatory policies.

Country Focus of the Policy

Although this volume sets out the broad sectoral strategy that will guide the Bank in water resources management, its application will need to be tailored to the situations and constraints facing individual countries. Many of the countries with limited renewable water resources are in the Middle East, North Africa, Central Asia, and Sub-Saharan Africa, the regions where populations are growing the fastest. Elsewhere, water scarcity is less of a problem at the national level but is nevertheless severe in many areas, for example, in northern China, western and southern India, western South America, and in large parts of Pakistan and Mexico. For some countries, such as those in Eastern Europe, pollution is the largest management problem. In much of Africa, implementation capacity is a critical issue and one of the key constraints in fashioning cost-effective solutions to water resource management problems that are exacerbated by frequent droughts. These regional and country differences will shape the design of country strategies and programs.

International Concerns about Water Resource Management

The Bank is not alone in raising concerns about the management of water resources. Many organizations in the United Nations and other development agencies are also concerned about the increasing scarcity of water and the need to protect natural resources and the environment (box 1-1). Among them, the Canadian International Development Agency, the French Ministry of Cooperation, the German Federal Ministry of Economic Cooperation and Development, the Overseas Development Administration (United Kingdom), and the U.S. Agency for International Development are developing, or have already developed, water resource strategies for foreign assistance.

The issue has also received attention in international forums. The 1990 Montreal International Forum "NGOs Working Together," for example, highlighted the problems of supplying drinking water and sanitation.

The delegates called for a new approach to managing water resources that emphasizes wide access to potable water and to sanitation, user participation and consultation, reliance on local community resources, the improvement and repair of existing systems, and a policy of comprehensive water resource management integrating environmental and economic considerations. More recently, in Delft, Dublin, and Rio de Janeiro, international conferences have highlighted the growing international consensus about the need to adopt comprehensive approaches to water resources management (box 1-2).

Box 1-2. The Dublin and Rio de Janeiro Conferences

The January 1992 International Conference on Water and the Environment: Development Issues for the 21st Century, held in Dublin, Ireland, called for new approaches to the assessment, development, and management of freshwater resources. The conference report sets out recommendations for action at the local, national, and international levels, based on four guiding principles. First, the effective management of water resources demands a holistic approach linking social and economic development with protection of natural ecosystems, including land and water linkages across catchment areas or groundwater aquifers. Second, water development and management should be based on a participatory approach involving users, planners, and policymakers at all levels. Third, women play a central part in providing, managing, and safeguarding water. Fourth, water has an economic value in all its competing uses and should be recognized as an economic good.

In June 1992, the United Nations Conference on Environment and Development in Rio de Janeiro, Brazil, confirmed the widespread consensus that the management of water resources needs to be reformed. The conference stated that, "The holistic management of freshwater as a finite and vulnerable resource, and the integration of sectoral water plans and programs within the framework of national economic and social policy, are of paramount importance for actions in the 1990s and beyond . . . . Integrated water resources management is based on the perception of water as an integral part of the ecosystem, a natural resource and social and economic good" (UNDP 1990:ch.18, p.3). The conference stressed "the implementation of allocation decisions through demand management, pricing mechanisms, and regulatory measures"(UNDP 1990:ch.18, p.5).

Organization of the Volume

Chapter 2 discusses the management problems that have beset the sector in many countries and how these are being aggravated by increasing demands for water and rising costs of new supplies. Chapter 3 outlines the strategy for improving the management of water resources. Chapter 4 spells out the role of the World Bank in helping countries implement better approaches to water resources management. Five appendixes discuss in detail market failures and public policy; lessons learned about the relation among water, people, and the environment; privatization and user participation; Bank guidelines related to water resources; and Bank experience with investments in water resources.

2

Conditions and Challenges in Managing Water Resources

Precipitation is the primary source of freshwater, with an annual flow about fifty times the normal stock held in lakes, rivers, and reservoirs. Annual precipitation can be highly variable, and withdrawal levels vary widely. The same area can experience drought one year and floods the next. Precipitation per capita is highest in Latin America and the Caribbean and lowest in the Middle East and North Africa. Withdrawals are highest in North America and lowest in Africa. Twenty-two countries today have renewable water resources of less than 1,000 cubic meters per capita, a level commonly taken to indicate a severe scarcity of water. An additional eighteen countries have less than 2,000 cubic meters per capita on average (dangerously little in years of short rainfall), and these levels are projected to decline further as population expands. Elsewhere, water scarcity is less of a problem at the national level, but it is nevertheless severe in certain regions, at certain times of the year, and during periods of drought. Worldwide, agriculture is by far the largest user of water: 69 percent is used by agriculture compared with 23 percent by industry and 8 percent by households. But in developing countries the share used by agriculture is even higher: 80 percent.

Problems of Management

Since water is critical for human survival, public authorities in most countries have assumed central responsibility for its overall management. This recognizes that reliance on market forces alone will not yield satisfactory outcomes, and some form of remedial government action is often required. Yet although governments may be involved for good reasons, their actions, when not properly formulated or implemented, often cause serious misallocations and waste of water resources. Three problems related to government activities are of particular concern: (a) fragmented public sector management that has neglected inter-dependencies among government agencies and jurisdictions; (b) reli-ance on overextended government agencies that have neglected financial accountability, user participation, and pricing while not deliv-ering services effectively to users and to the poor in particular; and (c) public investments and regulations that have neglected water quality, health, and environmental consequences. These problems are reviewed below.

Market failures

Given water's special characteristics, it is difficult to use unregulated markets to deliver water efficiently or to allocate it among sectors (box 2-1 and appendix A). Floods and droughts cause the availability of water to be highly variable, threatening life and incomes. This extreme vari-ability is difficult to manage equitably using only pricing and market mechanisms. Even more important, water moves through an intricate hydrological cycle of rainfall, absorption, runoff, and evapotranspira-tion that makes water activities highly interdependent and results in numerous externalities from various uses of surface and groundwater. Moreover, because of economies of scale and limited sources of water in many countries, the potential for monopoly control is high. Many of these problems of externalities and pricing can be corrected by appro-priate government policies that use market forces and incentives (for example, taxes, regulations, and enhancement of competitive pressures). Other problems (for example, public goods and inadequate private investments) may warrant public sector ownership and control of spe-cific activities (appendix A).

Fragmented management

Many governments face growing problems because they have failed to address water resources in a comprehensive manner. Government ac-tivities are generally organized so that each type of water use is managed by a separate department or agency—for example, irrigation, municipal water supply, power, and transportation—each responsible for its own operations and independent of the others. Issues related to the quantity and quality of water as well as health and environmental concerns are also considered separately, as are matters related to surface and ground-water. Problems of uncoordinated and fragmented decisionmaking

---

**Box 2-1. The Case for Government Involvement
in Water Management**

Water has several distinguishing characteristics that can result in market
failures and therefore define a role for public action.

- Large, lumpy capital requirements and economies of scale in
  water infrastructure tend to create natural monopolies, warrant-
  ing regulation to prevent overpricing. Moreover, many water
  investments produce joint products, such as recreation, electric
  power, flood control, and irrigation, which make pricing and
  allocation decisions difficult.
- The large size and extremely long time horizons of some investments, given underdeveloped capital markets and the potential
  for political interference in many water infrastructure investments, reduce the incentives for private investments in the sector;
  in such situations, public investments may be warranted.
- The uses of water within a river basin or aquifer are interdependent. Withdrawals in one part of the basin reduce the availability
  of water for other users; groundwater pumping by one user may
  lower the water table and increase pumping costs for all users;
  and pollution by one user affects others in the basin, especially
  those located downstream. These interdependencies suggest that
  having all users agree to the rules of the game—or lacking that,
  imposing government regulations, taxes, or both—could improve the social value of water resources.
- Certain aspects of water activities, such as the control of floods
  and waterborne diseases, are (local) public goods, which cannot
  easily be charged for on the basis of individual use. In such cases,
  public initiative may be required to ensure that levels of investment are appropriate.
- Water resources are often developed because of their strategic
  importance for national security and for regional development.
  Governments thus typically maintain ownership of water thor-
  oughfares, providing services such as the coast guard and traffic
  regulation.
- Some regions are subject to periodic droughts. Because water is
  essential to sustaining life, governments may take control of water

---

abound. Resolving these problems is particularly difficult in federal
governments, where states or provinces have jurisdiction over water in
their territory. In such cases, individual states may develop the same
water source without considering the impact on other states (box 2-2).
Similarly, domestic, industrial, and commercial supplies often are pro-

Box 2-2. Fragmented Management in South India

Water resources have been overdeveloped in a number of countries primarily due to fragmented decisionmaking. One example is the Chittar River in south India, whose highly variable flows have traditionally been diverted at many points into small reservoirs (tanks) used to irrigate the main rice crop following monsoon rains. Diversion channels are large to accommodate flows during floods. Thus, when a storage dam was constructed, the uppermost channel was able to absorb essentially all the regulated flow. The upper tanks now tend to remain full throughout the year, concentrating benefits and increasing evaporation losses. The more extensive lower areas have largely reverted to uncertain rainfed cultivation. Constructing the storage dam without adequately considering downstream users and the storage capacity already in the basin is a good example of how developing an individual project in isolation can cause significant economic losses.

The Sathanur Dam was constructed on the Ponnaiyar River in Tamil Nadu to serve a left bank command area, but it deprived the traditional and productive delta areas of irrigation water. The rights of downstream irrigators are recognized in the dam's operating rules, but most of the regulated flow below the dam is diverted into the upper channels. Losses have greatly increased in the wide sandy bed, and no surface water has reached the sea for twenty or more years. Continued spills in about 50 percent of all years were used to justify subsequent construction of the right bank irrigation command, further aggravating shortages in the delta and producing endless conflict between the two Sathanur commands. Moreover, additional storage dams on upstream tributaries are increasing evaporation losses in what was already a fully developed basin. High-return cropping has been replaced by cultivation on less productive lands served by tributaries that are inherently more variable than the main river was before the dam was built.

The Amaravati River is a tributary of the Cauvery, which is the most disputed major river in India. Without a Cauvery agreement, Karnataka (the upstream riparian state) has steadily developed massive irrigation schemes, depriving the delta (Tamil Nadu's rice bowl) of its accustomed supplies. Moreover, Tamil Nadu has been developing the Amaravati. As at Sathanur, releases are made from the Amaravati Dam for the traditional areas, but these areas are far downstream, and substituting regulated flows for flood flows has encouraged the development of private pumps along the river bank. New electric connections have now been banned, but little can be done to control illegal connections or diesel pumps, and little water now reaches the lowest command areas, let alone the Cauvery. Finally, new storage dams are being constructed on tributaries both in Kerala and Tamil Nadu, further depriving not only the old lands but also the new lands and the pump areas of water.

vided by local government units, which are not coordinated with pro-vincial or national water departments. This detachment may lead to situations in which different agencies are developing the same water source for different uses within an interdependent system.

Overextended government agencies

Given that water is essential for life, when it is scarce, governments tend to base allocations on political and social considerations rather than on purely economic criteria. Government involvement reflects the under-standable concern that relying exclusively on unregulated markets would not work. In many countries, the result has been a tradition of heavy dependence on centralized command and control administra-tions for developing and managing water resources and excessive reli-ance on government agencies to develop, operate, and maintain water systems. In many instances, this has stretched too thin the government's already limited implementation capacity. Moreover, in most cases users have not been consulted or otherwise involved in planning and manag-ing the water resources. The result has been a vicious cycle of unreliable projects that produce services that do not meet consumers' needs and for which they are unwilling to pay. The absence of financial discipline and accountability for performance—along with political interference in decisions about allocations and pricing—are reflected in a litany of problems: inefficient operations, inadequate maintenance, financial losses, and unreliable service delivery.

UNDERPRICING OF WATER. Pricing water well below its economic value is prevalent throughout the world. In many countries, expanding the supply is politically expedient, and therefore pricing and demand man-agement have received much less attention. The preference for expand-ing supply has led to investments in infrastructure that could have been avoided or postponed and that have increased the pressure on water-dependent ecosystems. Farmers in both industrial and developing coun-tries often pay little for their publicly supplied irrigation water. They have few incentives to refrain from growing water-intensive crops or to conserve water. For example, in some arid areas, water prices are so low that it is profitable to grow irrigated alfalfa, corn for silage (for example, in southern California), rice, and sugarcane. Similarly, many towns and cities charge fees that provide no incentive to conserve water; some charge nothing. A recent review of Bank-financed municipal water supply projects found that the price charged for water covered only about 35 percent of the average cost of supply, and charges in many irrigation systems are much less.

As a result of underpricing and other distorting policies, the value of water differs greatly among various uses in industrial and developing countries, often indicating gross misallocations if judged by economic criteria. In particular, agriculture, which absorbs the lion's share of water, often includes low-value uses per cubic meter compared with higher-value domestic and industrial uses. In California, for example, reallocating water from two agricultural areas to the metropolitan areas of San Francisco and Los Angeles would yield economic benefits of about $2 billion in 1990–2000.[1]

SERVICE DELIVERY TO THE POOR. Even after the International Drinking Water and Water Supply Decade, nearly 1 billion people in the developing world lack access to potable water, particularly the rural poor, and 1.7 billion must contend with inadequate sanitation facilities.[2] While the upper and middle classes often receive subsidized services, inefficient water operations have left little funding for extending services to the poor. Large numbers of poor people in urban areas depend on water vendors, paying at least ten times what a middle-class person pays for a liter of water (box 2-3). A review of vending in sixteen cities reported in the *World Development Report 1992* (World Bank 1992d) shows that the

---

Box 2-3. What Do the Poor Pay for Water?

Several studies show that the urban poor pay high prices for water supplies and spend a high proportion of their income on water. For example, in Port-au-Prince, Haiti, the poorest households sometimes spend 20 percent of their income on water; in Onitsha, Nigeria, the poor pay an estimated 18 percent of their income on water during the dry season compared with upper-income households who pay 2 to 3 percent; and in Addis Ababa, Ethiopia, and in Ukunda, Kenya, the urban poor spend up to 9 percent of their income on water. In Jakarta, Indonesia, of the 7.9 million inhabitants, only 14 percent of households receive water directly from the municipal system. Another 32 percent buy water from street vendors, who charge about $1.5 to $5.2 per cubic meter, depending on their distance from the public tap. In some cases, households purchasing from vendors pay as much as twenty-five to fifty times more per unit of water than households connected to the municipal system. Some examples of this phenomenon are found in Karachi, Pakistan; Port-au-Prince; Jakarta; Nouakchott, Mauritania; Dacca, Bangladesh; Tegucigalpa, Honduras; and Onitsha.

unit cost of vended water is much higher than that of water from a piped city supply—from 4 to 100 times higher, with a median of about 12.

Neglect of water quality, health, and the environment

Countries have generally paid too little attention to water quality and pollution control. In many developing countries, water supplies are of poor quality and are often unsafe for human consumption. Using polluted waters for human consumption is the principal cause of many health problems such as diarrheal diseases, which kill more than 3 million people each year—mostly children—and render sick more than a billion more. In addition to human suffering, water pollution causes devastating economic and environmental damage (box 2-4). Inadequately treated sewage aggravates poverty by polluting water-dependent food sources, engendering disease, and limiting access to safe drinking water. Furthermore, water-related diseases such as malaria, filariasis, and onchocerciasis are common in Sub-Saharan Africa. They are caused not by water pollution but by inadequate water management, poor hygiene, and lack of adequate public health education. These diseases have a debilitating impact on people and significant, negative consequences on productivity, particularly in rural areas. The discharge of untreated industrial waste, the runoff of agricultural chemicals, and poor land use practices in agriculture, forestry, and mining cause widespread degradation of land and water resources.

WATER POLLUTION. Many countries do not have standards to control water pollution adequately or the capacity to enforce existing legislation. In addition to pollution that is visible and degradable, new types of pollution have arisen involving small quantities of nondegradable synthetic chemicals that are invisible, toxic, persistent, and difficult and costly to treat. Although in recent years there has been improvement in the levels of water pollution in the industrial world, problems of water quality remain. In the United States, almost 50 percent of the waterways are still impaired by pollution, as are many of the major rivers and near-shore waters of Great Britain, Japan, and Scandinavia. In France and Germany, despite decades of collecting pollution effluent charges, the Rhine, Rhone, and Seine rivers remain polluted.

ENVIRONMENTAL IMPACT OF PROJECTS. Many public investment projects have adversely affected the quality of water and contributed to the degradation of aquatic ecosystems. In part, this has resulted because piecemeal evaluations of water resource projects have often overlooked the cumulative environmental degradation caused by several projects and because the interactions within the ecosystem have not been adequately considered. The misuse of land, particularly in agriculture, forestry, and mining, has resulted not only in the sedimentation of waterways and water pollution but also in poverty—as lands fail and families are forced to relocate, often to overcrowded cities. Because many

---

Box 2-4. Economic and Environmental Consequences of Inadequate Sanitation

Although funding for water supply projects receives attention, too often adequate sanitation does not. Large amounts of new water are brought into urban areas, which creates large amounts of untreated, polluted wastewater that is often used by the urban poor. This not only perpetuates disease but also creates larger environmental problems downriver, especially when sanitation projects include only the collection of sewage without adequate treatment. In developing nations, high economic costs are associated with the practice of boiling water as well as with the treatment of diseases, such as the Hepatitis A outbreak in Shanghai or the recent cholera outbreaks in Brazil and Peru. In Peru, more than 1,000 people died from cholera, and losses in agricultural exports and tourism revenues were estimated at close to $1 billion. In 1991, polluted water from Amman's poor sewage works and industrial effluents severely damaged 6,000 hectares of land downriver used for irrigated vegetable crops.

In Colombia, cleaning up the Bogotá River would cost an estimated $1.4 billion. In Shanghai, the cost of moving intakes upstream, because of pollution, is $300 million, while in Lima, upstream pollution of the Rimac River has increased treatment costs by 30 percent.

A recent review of the World Bank's experience with 120 water supply and sanitation projects found that, while 104 projects funded water supply, only 58 included a sanitation component. Also sanitation components within projects were often eliminated because of cost overruns. In only a few of the cities with Bank-financed water supply projects was adequate sewer or sanitation provided to handle the increased wastewater created by the project. The review concluded that the Bank and its borrowers have not adequately invested in the removal and treatment of sewage. Diseases will continue to spread among the poor, and the economic and environmental deterioration will continue until adequate wastewater disposal accompanies the provision of water. Improved low-cost and more appropriate technologies are now available to mitigate the high costs of conventional sewerage and sewage disposal systems.

irrigation projects lack drainage components, they have caused water-logging and concentrated large quantities of salts that have severely damaged irrigated land around the world. Moreover, when water is diverted upstream for irrigation and other uses, downstream areas that support sensitive water-dependent ecosystems, including wetlands, become less able to fulfill their valuable functions, such as filtering pollutants and supporting biodiversity. Important river fisheries have been eliminated by such diversions, and important deltas have been impaired by low flows. Some development projects have deprived poor people, particularly the rural poor, of access to water of adequate quality and quantity to sustain them and their economic activities. This has occurred when traditional riverine communities have not participated in planning and implementing projects and when their needs have not been

---

Box 2-5. Water Scarcity in Jordan

Water resources in Jordan are scarce and expensive to exploit. Jordan's economy has been transformed since the early 1950s, when its population was only 0.6 million, with agriculture largely confined to rainfed farming and livestock raising. Population (currently 3.2 million, increasing at 3.8 percent annually), increasing urbanization (currently 70 percent of the population), and rising incomes have increased the demand for water. Approximately 48,500 hectares have been brought under irrigation in the Jordan Valley, the northern highlands, and southeastern Jordan. This has raised concerns about the balance of water use between irrigation and municipal and industrial purposes. The strategy in the past has been to use surface water principally for irrigation and groundwater both for municipal and industrial uses and for irrigation. This strategy has been rational because groundwater is of better quality and is concentrated in the uplands, where most of the population lives.

Municipal and industrial water currently accounts for about 25 percent of total water use, and water consumption is modest for a country with Jordan's per capita income. Water is metered, and charges are high by the region's standards. However, since the population is expected to increase from 3.2 million in 1990 to 7.4 million in 2015, even with modest consumption rates, the demand for municipal and industrial water is expected to increase, so that by 2015 it will account for about 40 percent of total demand for water. In response to the growing scarcity of water, irrigation is now done by sprinkler and drip pressure pipe systems, which have largely replaced less efficient systems.

incorporated in them. Large cities such as Bangkok and Mexico City are dangerously depleting their groundwater supplies. In some areas of Bangkok, overpumping of groundwater has caused an annual subsidence rate of 14 centimeters, which worsens floods and destroys infrastructure (appendix B).

Trends in Demand and Supply

Against this background of mismanagement and waste, population is growing rapidly, and with it the demand for water. At the same time, the cost of tapping new sources of water is also rising. These trends will aggravate the water management problems outlined above (box 2-5).

Three underexploited sources of water remain in Jordan, two of which are shared internationally: water that would be made available by the construction of a storage facility on the Yarmouk River, known as the Wehdah Dam; water from the Disi aquifer in southeastern Jordan; and treated sewage effluent, which will be increasingly available, collected, and reused for irrigation. Water planning strategies in the 1980s envisaged using all the water from the proposed Wehdah Dam for irrigation, thus permitting more land to be irrigated in the Jordan Valley. Licenses were also granted to develop the Disi aquifer for irrigated agriculture. Increasing awareness of water scarcities, however, caused this strategy to be revised. It was realized that the Disi aquifer should be regarded as a strategic reserve, to be used for municipal and industrial water as the need arose, and that "mining" it for agriculture was not in the interests of the country. Yet this future source of municipal and industrial water may be saved only if an international agreement can be reached by countries using the aquifer.

Even with rational planning and allocation of Jordan's water, all known water sources within Jordanian territory would be fully used by 2015, and about one-third of the irrigation water in the Jordan Valley would consist of treated effluent. After that, the alternatives would be to reduce irrigated area, to demineralize the water, or to import water from other countries (such as through the proposed Turkish "peace" pipeline). Jordan is not the only country in this region to face critical water shortages, but it is one of the first to appreciate the seriousness of the problem and to seek new strategic solutions.

Population growth

Population growth and urbanization are key factors underlying the enormous growth in the demand for water and the increased environmental degradation. Under the most optimistic scenario, the world's population is expected to grow from 5.3 billion in 1990 to 6.2 billion by 2000 and to at least 8 billion by 2025. This will increase the demand for food supplies and thus for new and improved systems of irrigated agricultural production. The growth in population, some 90 percent of which will occur in urban areas, will also increase the demand for water of quality suitable for domestic and industrial use and for treatment of wastes. But the existing systems of urban water supply and sanitation in many countries already fail to provide adequate services, and thus the problems posed by pollution are likely to grow. Urbanization and industrialization will also increase the demand for energy and hydropower. These developments pose a great challenge for governments in their management of water resources in the coming decades.

Box 2-6. The Increasing Costs of Supplying Water

Many cities convey water over long distances and use high-cost pumping extensively. In addition, intensive use of water has created the need for additional treatment because the quality of the new source is poor or the original source was rejected because the damage to its quality was irreversible. In the following examples the figures do not include the cost of treatment and distribution.

- Amman, Jordan. When the water supply system was based on groundwater, the average incremental cost was estimated to be $0.41 per cubic meter, but chronic shortages of groundwater led to the use of surface water. This raised the average incremental cost to $1.33 per cubic meter. The most recent works involve pumping water up 1,200 meters from a site about 40 kilometers from the city. The next scheme contemplates the construction of a dam and a conveyor, at an estimated cost of $1.50 per cubic meter, which is also about the cost of desalinating seawater, $1 to $2 per cubic meter.
- Shenyang, China. The cost of new water supplies will rise from $0.04 to $0.11 per cubic meter, almost a 200 percent increase, between 1988 and 2000. The main reason is that the quality of groundwater from the Hun Valley Alluvium, the current water source, is not good enough for potable water. As a result, water will have to be conveyed to Shenyang by gravity from a surface

---

Cost of new water supplies

Even with measures to contain the growth in demand and to improve the efficiency of existing systems, new water supplies will be needed for many urban areas. However, the lowest cost and most reliable sources of water have already been developed in many countries. The new sources of supply currently being considered have higher financial and environmental costs than those developed earlier. The costs of municipal water supply and irrigation will increase even further when adequate drainage and sanitation facilities are included as essential parts of these investments. The authorities in Beijing, for example, may have to obtain badly needed water from a source more than 1,000 kilometers away, while those in Mexico City must consider expensive schemes to pump water over a height of 2,000 meters. For other cities, the cost of a cubic meter of water provided by "the next project" can be two to three times the cost of current supplies (box 2-6), even before environmental costs are factored in. In fact, the cost may be so high in some cities that

---

source 51 kilometers from the city. In Yingkou the average incremental cost of water diverted from the nearby Daliao River is about $0.16 per cubic meter. However, because of the heavy pollution, this source cannot be used for domestic purposes. As a result, water is currently being transported into the city from the more distant Liu River at a cost of $0.30 per cubic meter.

- Lima, Peru. During 1981 the average incremental cost of a project to meet short- and medium-term needs, based in part both on a surface source from the Rimac River and on groundwater supplies, was $0.25 per cubic meter. Since the aquifer has been severely depleted, groundwater sources cannot be used to satisfy needs beyond the early 1990s. To meet long-term urban needs, a transfer of water from the Atlantic watershed is being planned, at an estimated average incremental cost of $0.53 per cubic meter.

- Mexico City, Mexico. Water is currently being pumped over an elevation of 1,000 meters into the Mexico Valley from the Cutzamala River through a pipeline about 180 kilometers long. The average incremental cost of water from this source is $0.82 per cubic meter, almost 55 percent more than the previous source, the Mexico Valley aquifer. The aquifer has been restricted due to the problems of land subsidence, the lowered water table, and the deteriorated water quality. The newly designed water supply project for the city is expected to be even more costly, since it will have a longer transmission line and water will be pumped over an elevation of 2,000 meters.

desalinization will become a viable option for potable water. The same trend can be found in irrigation, where the real cost of new large-scale irrigation systems has been increasing.

International Water Resources

International watercourses are a classic case in which national interests among countries are likely to diverge because of externalities. Given the international context, however, inefficiency caused by interdependent water uses cannot be resolved through a single government's policies. Upstream countries see little benefit from increasing or maintaining the flow and quality of water for those downstream. Without enforceable international water-use rights established by treaty, countries make decisions without considering the consequences for other countries using the same resource. However, securing such international agreements is often difficult. The end result may be environmental, social, and economic losses in the downstream countries that are greater than the benefits to the upstream country.

Scope of the Problem

More than 200 river basins are shared by two or more countries. These basins account for about 60 percent of the earth's land area. Fragmented planning and development of the associated transboundary river, lake, and coastal basins is the rule rather than the exception. Although more than 300 treaties have been signed by countries to deal with specific concerns about international water resources and more than 2,000 treaties have provisions related to water, coordinated management of international river basins is still rare, resulting in economic losses, environmental degradation, and international conflict.

Institutional and Political Challenges

Countries guard their perceived water rights. Treaties notwithstanding, many have not devoted funding to manage these surface and subsurface water resources jointly. Data are not shared freely among nations, and cooperation is often lacking. As a result, water disputes over quantity allocations remain unresolved, and additional concerns are now arising over the effects that poor water quality and low flows have on aquatic ecosystems.

Groundwater

International water issues also involve important groundwater resources. In a number of cases, aquifers cross international boundaries; thus pumping by one country interferes with another country's pumping or stream flows. Assessing the effects on riparian countries of overpumping in different areas of a deep aquifer is, however, often technically difficult.

Notes

1. A billion is 1,000 million. All dollar amounts are U.S. dollars.

2. The United Nations General Assembly proclaimed 1981–90 to be the International Drinking Water and Water Supply Decade. During this time, national and international efforts were made to expand access to potable water and adequate sanitation. Despite much progress, initial goals for service delivery were not met. Access to safe water expanded from 77 to 82 percent and from 30 to 63 percent of the population in urban and rural areas, respectively. Also, access to adequate sanitation increased from 69 to 72 percent and from 37 to 49 percent of the urban and rural residents, respectively. This increase in the percentage of population served occurred during a period when the population of the developing world increased 23 percent. But the growth in population, combined with funding limitations, inadequate cost recovery, improper operations and maintenance, and lack of trained staff prevented these efforts from reaching the goals set by the international community at the beginning of the decade.

3

Improving Water Resources Management

The challenges and weaknesses outlined in chapter 2 require a renewed emphasis on improving the management of water resources based on sound policies and strengthened institutional arrangements. This approach has two guiding principles. First, water resource management policies and activities should be formulated within the context of a comprehensive analytical framework that takes into account the interdependencies among sectors and protects aquatic ecosystems. Such a framework would guide the establishment of improved coordination among institutions, consistent regulations, coherent policies, and targeted government actions. Second, efficiency in water management must be improved through the greater use of pricing and through greater reliance on decentralization, user participation, privatization, and financial autonomy to enhance accountability and improve performance incentives. Water services to the poor require special attention. At the same time, systems for protecting and restoring water and environmental resources need to be established. Furthermore, international agencies, such as the World Bank, can play a larger role in helping developing countries to improve the management of their international water resources.

Comprehensive Approach

The primary roles of the public sector are to define and implement a strategy for managing water resources; to provide an appropriate legal, regulatory, and administrative framework; to guide intersectoral allocations; and to develop water resources in the public domain. Investments, policies, and regulations in one part of a river basin or in one sector affect activities throughout the basin. Thus, these decisions need to be formulated in the context of a broad strategy that takes the long-term view, incorporates assumptions about the actions and reactions of all participants in water management, and fully considers the ecosystems and socioeconomic structures that exist in a river basin. This is an indicative planning process for dealing with cross-sectoral issues. The goal is to ensure the sustainability of the water environment for multiple uses as an integral part of a country's economic development process. The level of complexity of the strategy will differ among countries, depending on their problems, resources, priorities, and capacities. Its execution and management should involve the public sector, private enterprises, and water user groups; its degree of decentralization will depend on each country's capabilities.

Analytical framework

At the heart of the approach is the development of a comprehensive analytical framework for water resources management. Water resources should be managed in the context of a national water strategy that reflects the nation's social, economic, and environmental objectives and is based on an assessment of the country's water resources. The assessment would include a realistic forecast of the demand for water, based on projected population growth and economic development, and a consideration of options for managing demand and supply, taking into account existing investments and those likely to occur in the private sector. The strategy would spell out priorities for providing water services; establish policies on water rights, water pricing and cost recovery, public investment, and the role of the private sector in water development; and institute measures for environmental protection and restoration. The framework would facilitate the consideration of relationships between the ecosystem and socioeconomic activities in river basins. In essence, this comprehensive approach breaks down very complex problems in a river basin into more manageable elements to achieve coherent cross-sectoral water management. Alternative public investment options and patterns of water management can be considered and evaluated, especially in light of supply and land use interdependencies and of the major social and environmental consequences that characterize water resource sector investments or reallocations.

Although the complexity of the analysis will vary with the circumstances, it is often possible to clarify priorities and to take account of key interdependencies, using relatively uncomplicated frameworks. Once a suitable overall framework has been formulated, individual projects can be more easily designed to fit the country's objectives without adding unnecessary complexities. The analytical framework provides the underpinnings for formulating public policy. Regulations governing pollution, health standards, and environmental protection address water quality interdependencies among users. Appropriate pricing and charging systems (and water markets where feasible) must be established that provide the correct signals so that decentralized decisionmaking can improve the allocation of resources. Within a decentralized system, adequate charges would also endow water entities with operational and financial autonomy to provide reliable and sustainable services. In general, countries should move toward decentralizing the delivery of water services, to the extent possible, and toward using appropriate pricing to create the preconditions for efficient, sustainable delivery of water services.

Public water investments

Specific options for investment and development must consider the interrelations among different sources of water. Surface and groundwater resources are physically linked, so their management and development should also be linked. Land and water management activities as well as issues of quantity and quality need to be integrated within basins or watersheds, so that upstream and downstream linkages are recognized and activities in one part of the river basin take into account their impact on other parts. Investments in infrastructure may displace people and disturb ecosystems. Thus, water resource assessments need to consider these cross-sectoral implications.[1]

Where noneconomic objectives (such as biodiversity, food security, and equity) preclude fully using the economic value of water to guide decisions, the need for transparency in decisionmaking would be served by measuring the economic costs (in terms of economic benefits forgone) of satisfying these objectives. A proper evaluation of costs would also take into account the possibility of implementation problems and environmental costs and risks, including the costs of relocating people and restoring their sources of livelihood as well as the estimated costs of ecological damage.[2] Many types of models have been developed to aid these evaluations. Selection of a model should be guided by determining its prime use at the outset. Careful interpretation and judgment concerning how modeling results are to be used are also essential elements of successful planning and decisionmaking.

Opportunity cost of water

An important tool that can be derived from the comprehensive analytical framework is the opportunity cost of water. It provides a measure of the scarcity value of water to society, thus highlighting any cross-sectoral differences in value, taking into account society's multiple objectives and water's multiple uses and interdependencies. If economic criteria alone are employed, water should be allocated to a given use when the opportunity cost is lower than the value of the selected use. Determining the opportunity cost of water requires information about, and analysis of, future demand, supply options, investment alternatives, and the economic costs of pollution and other environmental damage. In turn, the opportunity cost can help to guide the price structure for sales to decentralized distribution entities, to evaluate the economic viability of investment proposals, to establish the magnitude of the penalties to be imposed on polluters, and to guide cross-sectoral allocations of water.

Information needs

In many cases, inadequate and unreliable data constitute a serious constraint to developing and implementing a country's water resource strategy and to managing water effectively. For a country to make sound decisions about water management—especially in the context of large investment projects and real-time management of the resource at the level of the basin or watershed—a considerable amount of information is required. Of course, the appropriate degree of detail and sophistication of information systems needs to be determined in the context of the specific country and river basin. In general, a long-term demand forecast, with a time horizon compatible with the type of project involved (for example, the lifetime of most dams and open channel delivery systems exceeds fifty years), is needed, as are adequate assessments of water resources and environmental impacts. Equally important are current data concerning water supply and demand conditions so critical for efficient day-to-day management. To meet these information needs, countries should (a) define information requirements for national water resources, taking particular account of the multiple demands for water; (b) review institutional arrangements linking the providers and users of data; (c) identify and implement new mechanisms for funding hydrological services, where such mechanisms are required to provide adequate financial resources; (d) select appropriate technologies for collecting data, particularly data on water quality and on groundwater, and for implementing user-friendly data management systems; (e) establish national data banks for information on water resources; and (f) define the human resources needed for hydrological information systems and provide education and training to meet those needs.

Institutional and Regulatory Systems

An institutional setting should be created within an effective legal and regulatory framework to facilitate cross-sectoral actions that contribute to improved management of water resources. Institutional reform should be responsive to traditional norms and practices and should, to the extent possible, integrate these within the new structures. In many cases, regulatory systems and coordination structures exist but function poorly because they lack authority and the appropriate resources for enforcement. Changes in legislation to ensure that regulations are coordinated and enforced may thus be necessary ingredients of institutional reform.

Legal and regulatory framework

Legislation provides the basis for government action in the regulatory and operational areas and establishes the context for action by nongovernmental entities and individuals. In many countries, surface water belongs to the state, subject to varying recognition of historical private or local rights. In addition, the state is often charged with holding in public trust, and managing for the common good, aquatic living resources. Governments authorize water use, but allocations and priorities are often vaguely stated or are absent, and many uses (such as instream or environmental uses) may be overlooked. Often the procedures to be followed in reallocating water to higher-priority or higher-valued purposes are not explicitly stated; thus reallocations may not take place or may follow ad hoc decisions at a high cost. Governments should clearly indicate priorities for reallocations and establish practical rules for handling the year-to-year variability in precipitation and availability of water. The rights to water need to be clearly defined, with due concern shown for the interests of indigenous people, the poor, and other disadvantaged groups. The legal basis for water user associations also needs to be established both for agriculture and for domestic water supply and sanitation.

The prevalence of social concerns, environmental externalities, and the tendency toward natural monopoly in water services mean that effective regulatory systems are prerequisites for decentralized management. Regulatory systems monitor and enforce established laws, agreements, rules, and standards. Among subjects covered to varying degrees are the administration of water rights and allocations, standards of service, water quality and environmental protection, prices charged by regulated utilities, competitiveness of entry to water service industries, and the financial viability of public utilities. In many countries regulatory functions are weak and are formulated and enforced inconsistently by different agencies. The need for coordination and coherence in formulating regulations should be addressed by applying a comprehensive analytical approach.

Coordination structures

Most countries have a multiplicity of public agencies and commissions with overlapping responsibilities for managing water resources. Because public agencies typically focus on only one type of water use, decisionmaking tends to be fragmented. Different agencies often have conflicting plans to develop the same publicly owned water resources. Pricing policies also may be inconsistent, leading to the misuse of water resources. Institutional arrangements thus need to be developed that encourage water-related agencies to coordinate and establish mutually agreed upon priorities and policies for investment, regulation, and allocation, especially for the management of river basins. River basin organizations can be an effective means for coordination when they have adequate authority and financial autonomy. Other alternatives include establishing coordinating committees, with representatives from major public water agencies. Such committees could have responsibility for reviewing and recommending changes in investments and management to promote the overall water resources strategy and achieve consistency within each river basin. To coordinate activities at the national level, committees may need to be set up in planning or finance ministries and have adequate authority to monitor and review water activities and to enforce consistency with national strategies. An important principle in assigning responsibility is that policy, planning, and regulatory functions must be separated from operational functions at each level of government.

RESOLUTION OF INTERSTATE CONFLICTS. In countries with a federal structure, interstate (interprovincial) conflicts over the management of shared water resources are inevitable. Hence, methods are needed for deciding among mutually exclusive proposals and for judging among conflicting claims for water rights. In some countries, interstate river basin organizations have been set up for this purpose. If endowed with adequate authority under suitable legal provisions, such organizations can be effective in resolving disputes. Another approach is to rely on interstate agreements, which are enforceable under the country's legal system. A joint commission that guides individual state operating entities is often acceptable, subject to ultimate resolution of remaining disagreements through the legal system.

COUNTRY EXAMPLES. Some developing countries—for example, Mexico and Tunisia—have begun to reform their water management systems in the direction outlined above; some industrial countries have experience with even more ambitious coordination schemes. The French system, for example, has operated effectively for twenty-five years (box 3-1). It uses river basin committees to decide on long-term plans for developing water resources. Regulation and enforcement are conducted by various national ministries, while the operation and maintenance of different components of the water system are left primarily to regulated private

---

Box 3-1. The French System of Managing River Basins

An important aspect of the French system is that water resources are managed at the level of the river basin. There are six river basin committees and six river basin financial agencies, whose territories closely correspond to the main river basins. They specialize in water resource management (planning and macromanagement), which they have performed efficiently for twenty-five years. The river basin committees facilitate coordination among all the parties involved in managing water resources. These committees have become the center for negotiations and policymaking at the river basin level. To formulate action plans, the river basin financial agencies generate and use extensive data on the current and targeted quality and quantity of water and industrial effluents. A center of technical expertise and knowledge about water resources used by government agencies and other interested parties, they have become the primary planning institution for river basins.

The committees approve the long-term (twenty to twenty-five year) schemes for developing water resources. Every five years they vote on action plans to improve water quality. In addition, they vote annually on two fees to be paid by water users within the river basin: one fee based on the level of water consumed and the other one on the level of pollution at each point source. These two fees encourage environmentally sound behavior in water use and provide financial incentives (grants or soft loans) to achieve the five-year action plan. The committees are composed of 60 to 110 persons, who represent interested parties: the national administration, regional and local governments, industrial and agricultural groups, and citizens. The financial agencies implement the policies set by the committees in their basins; they, in turn, propose the long-term scheme to develop water resources, the five-year plan, and the level of water fees and incentives. They also collect fees, extend grants and loans, make midterm plans, collect and process data, conduct studies, and finance research programs.

sector entities and public utilities. In the United States, the Tennessee Valley Authority plays an important role in coordinating agencies in implementing a comprehensive approach to water resource management throughout the river basin (appendix B).

Incentives

As indicated in chapter 2, a major weakness of past approaches to the water sector has been the excessive reliance on overextended government agencies to manage water resources. The unsatisfactory performance of these agencies has caused many countries to rethink their organizational arrangements and to seek efficiency gains through decentralization and greater reliance on pricing and incentives.

Pricing and demand management

The importance of pricing and other incentives that encourage consumers to adopt efficient water-use practices depends on the relative value of the water. When good-quality water is plentiful—and cheap—it does not pay to invest in costly monitoring devices and pricing systems. However, because demand is responsive to price, it becomes increasingly worthwhile to measure, monitor, and price water carefully as it becomes scarce. In many areas of the world, underpricing has caused serious misuse of water.

DIFFERENT VALUES IN URBAN AND AGRICULTURAL USES. As noted in chapter 2 and the *World Development Report 1992* (World Bank 1992d), in most countries, urban and agricultural entitlements have separately determined sectoral water allocations. Although these allocations may have been appropriate historically, subsequent developments may change their economic implications. Thus, in many areas, the much higher value of water in domestic and industrial uses, compared with agricultural uses, indicates a high economic cost of the existing allocation.

REALLOCATING WATER. Reallocating water to increase aggregate economic benefits could be accomplished in principle through three mechanisms: (a) administrative reallocation by government decree, (b) trading among users, and (c) setting higher prices for water so that low-value users would release water for higher-value users. The information requirements are likely to be higher with the administrative reallocation and price setting approaches, than with trading, in which participants have incentives to seek the most beneficial adjustments based on information they already possess. The transfer of water under each of these three mechanisms entails third-party effects, whereby groups that benefit indirectly from the original allocation (for example, service industries catering to agriculture or downstream users benefiting from return flows) suffer economic losses and thus may require compensation and mechanisms for adjustment. This would be of particular concern when the groups adversely affected are the poor. A similar concern arises for farmers when water is transferred by administrative decision or in response to higher charges because farmers lose an economic rent they perceive as an acquired right. Indeed, the political leverage of farmers often blocks reallocation even in situations of gross misallocations. An approach based on trading may avoid the political debate while improving the allocation, but other costs must be considered as well. Environmental concerns (which are not reflected in market transactions) would need to be satisfied with any transfer. Similarly, physical adjustment and conveyance costs will need to be borne in any reallocation, but the construction of new conveyance systems to facilitate transfer is easier when governments can invoke the privilege of eminent domain to obtain the right-of-way.

TRANSACTION COSTS OF REALLOCATION. An important factor affecting most water trading is the transaction cost associated with organizing the large number of original beneficiaries (in most cases, farmers) to agree collectively on the quantities and terms of the trade. Some of these organizational costs also arise in the case of efficiency pricing since the difficulties of charging individual farmers in many large irrigation systems are best overcome by relying on user associations. Because cross-sectoral reallocations are typically feasible if done in bulk (rather than through individual transactions), trading often depends on collective action. It also depends on the original recipients possessing transferable rights to water. Other necessary institutional arrangements include appropriate regulatory and legal systems to monitor and address environmental concerns and third-party issues. Trading water within a sector is common in many countries, but trading among sectors has been documented only in the western United States and Chile, and its extent and impact have not been sufficiently explored. Additional experimentation with water trading in developing countries is needed to determine when and to what extent it can improve social welfare under existing institutional capacities and to formulate complementary legal, regulatory, and institutional arrangements. Where trading cannot be established, alternative mechanisms, including pricing and direct allocations, are required if a country is to obtain the benefits of transferring water from low- to high-value uses. In such circumstances, sectoral pricing and reallocation decisions should be made using a comprehensive analytical framework that considers national objectives. Adjustments to achieve compatible prices among urban and agricultural users, reflecting the opportunity cost of water, can help guide sectoral allocations on the basis of the revealed preferences of water users.[3]

PRICES FOR URBAN AND INDUSTRIAL USE. Charging fees for domestic and industrial water supplies is generally straightforward. In most cases, use can be metered, and fees can be charged according to the volume and reliability of water used. Economic efficiency would be obtained by setting water charges equal to the opportunity cost of water. However, immediate adoption of such prices often proves to be politically difficult. Thus, given the low level of cost recovery at present and the extent of underpricing, fees that establish the water entity's financial autonomy would be a good starting point to ensure the entity's independence and the sustainability of operations. Both public and private entities should pay for the costs of the water and sanitation services they receive.

POVERTY ALLEVIATION. Research and experience indicate that when water services are reliable, the poor are willing to pay for them and that when service is not reliable, the poor pay more for less, typically from street vendors. As pointed out in the *World Development Report 1992* (World Bank 1992d), the poor need to be provided with a wider range of options so they can choose the level of water services for which they are willing to pay, thereby giving suppliers a financial stake in meeting the needs of the poor. Fee schedules can be structured so that consumers receive a limited amount of water at a low cost and pay a higher fee for additional water. Fees set in this manner can correspond to efficiency prices for incremental consumption, even as they provide low base rates that benefit the poor. However, the schedule in aggregate should provide for full cost recovery; otherwise, the financial viability of the water entity is endangered. Another form of subsidy to the poor, which may be handled through one-time budgetary transactions, is a subsidy for connecting households to the water supply and sanitation network. Moreover, increased attention needs to be given, through public health education, to the handling of water within the home and school to ensure that good-quality water is not contaminated through poor hygiene. Special attention should be given to rural areas, where most of the poor live, and emphasis should be placed on providing the rural poor with access to a reliable supply of adequate-quality water.

FEES FOR IRRIGATION. For irrigation, as for domestic and industrial use, prices reflecting opportunity costs are desirable, but cost recovery fees that ensure financial viability of water entities are a more realistic immediate objective. Since such fees are often significantly lower than the opportunity cost, they reduce, but do not eliminate, the misuse of water resources. Therefore, in the interim, other mechanisms such as water trading or administrative reallocation are needed. The evidence suggests that farmers want, and are willing to pay for, reliable supplies of irrigated water (box 3-2). However, the practical problems of pricing for irrigation services are sometimes quite complex. For example, in large irrigation systems in South Asia, hundreds of thousands of farmers receive varying degrees of service in areas covering more than 1 million hectares. It is difficult, and in many of these very large systems extremely costly, to measure the volume of water each farmer receives. Many irrigation agencies cannot even identify all the farmers who receive water.

COST RECOVERY THROUGH USER GROUPS. One way to circumvent the costs of metering individual use is to measure the water delivered to an entire village or water user association, which is, in turn, responsible for delivering water to farmers and collecting fees. Under such an approach, the user association monitors use and determines household fees, with

---

Box 3-2. Can the Poor Pay for Irrigated Water?

Information on communal and private irrigation systems in various countries in Asia shows that even very poor farmers will pay high fees for good-quality and reliable irrigation services.

- In Bangladesh, it is not uncommon for farmers to agree to pay 25 percent of their dry season irrigated rice crop to the owners of nearby tubewells who supply their water.
- In Nepal, studies of farmer-owned and -managed irrigation systems have revealed that farmers contribute large amounts of cash and labor to pay the annual cost of operations and maintenance. For example, in six hill systems studied in detail, the average annual labor contribution was sixty-eight days per hectare. In one thirty-five-hectare system, annual labor contributions were approximately fifty days per hectare, while cash assessments averaged the equivalent of more than one month of labor.

Although many of these farmers are very poor in an absolute sense, they are willing to pay for good-quality irrigation services that raise and stabilize their income. Thus, the critical issue is providing these poor farmers with reliable, profitable, and sustainable irrigation services.

Box 3-3. Modern Irrigation Systems in North Africa

Modern irrigation systems using hydraulically self-operated devices were developed in water-scarce North Africa in the late 1940s following an intensive hydraulics research program. These devices were in general use for irrigation schemes constructed in Algeria, Morocco, and Tunisia during the 1950s. Except for areas of traditional irrigation, most modern schemes have the following characteristics:

* Water is delivered under arranged demand to individual farmers.
* Farm size is generally between two and five hectares.
* Main canals are operated under upstream or downstream control, or a combination of these two methods, and the distribution system is operated under upstream control.

Such capital-intensive systems are economically viable in countries where the demand for water is high relative to the supply. These systems allow countries to charge water users according to the volume of water delivered and to pursue pricing policies that encourage conservation and efficient use of water. Some of these irrigation techniques have been transferred to the Middle East and, in isolated and pilot projects, to other developing countries.

---

the authorities (or the contractor operating the system) determining, in consultation with the association, how much water is to be delivered to the village and at what price. This approach uses the ability of local organizations to monitor use and to apply peer pressure for collecting fees. Experience shows, however, that such pressure works best when the association is strong enough to bear the tensions that may be created.

VOLUMETRIC CHANGES. In systems with more control, the water delivered to each farm can be measured, and charges can be based on its volume and reliability, thus encouraging the more economical use of water (box 3-3). Such systems are expensive. Nevertheless, in many areas water is so scarce that the benefits of pricing and demand management strategies—encouraging greater operational efficiency and reallocating water to higher-value uses—outweigh the transaction costs associated with their introduction.

INDIRECT METHODS OF SETTING IRRIGATION CHARGES. Other approaches to levying charges do not rely on direct measurement of water use. Such measures are less effective than individual volumetric charges, but in most cases they do provide some incentives for using water more efficiently. Given their limited implementation costs, they are often the best approach, especially when water is plentiful and relatively cheap. The simplest approach is to estimate the amount of water delivered based on the number of hectares irrigated. Such per hectare charges do not provide an incentive to conserve water; hence, they do little to promote efficient use. However, they do provide a basis for financial autonomy and independence of the system.[4] Alternative measures that better reflect the quantity of water used (or the value of irrigation services provided) include varying the per hectare water charges by the type of crop grown, by the number of irrigation periods in a season, or by the length of irrigation time.

WATER CONSERVATION. An important element of any strategy designed to deal with water is incentives for adopting technologies and management approaches to make the use, allocation, and distribution of water more efficient. Water fees and fiscal incentives can encourage firms to adopt water-saving technologies, including water reuse systems. Such technologies and management approaches make it easier to conserve water, to increase the efficiency of water use and conveyance, and to reuse wastewater. Similarly, water fees can provide incentives for farmers to shift into crops that use less water. As water scarcity and waste disposal problems become more acute, it will become increasingly important to adopt and improve water conservation practices, desalinization and wastewater reuse systems, and overall pollution-reduction approaches. Moreover, there will also be a greater potential for community-based water and sewage systems and for private sector involvement in these systems, if the scale of the technology is reduced. Small-scale, low-cost technologies are especially needed for rural water supplies in the developing world. If the technology does not have major capital requirements, community groups and small private enterprises will be better able to provide water and sewage services. Attention should also be given to developing and diffusing technologies that use groundwater resources more efficiently because water is becoming increasingly scarce in many arid areas.

DEMAND MANAGEMENT. Besides price-based incentives to conserve water, demand management includes educational, technical, and administrative programs. Often these are used together with price incentives to conserve water and thus limit the need for new supplies. Technical measures include dual plumbing systems that handle two qualities of water and toilets, faucets, and irrigation equipment designed to use less water (see box 3-3 on North African irrigation technology and box 3-4 on municipal initiatives). Administrative controls include ration-

Box 3-4. Demand Management Programs for Municipal Water Supply

In their efforts to limit the need for increased water supplies, many municipalities have employed demand management programs.

- The city of Bogor, Indonesia, was faced with high investment costs of developing additional water supplies. The municipal authorities decided to substantially cut the water consumption levels of domestic and commercial consumers. Water fees were increased initially by approximately 30 percent, resulting in an average decrease in consumption of 29 percent. This action was followed by a campaign to reduce water use further, particularly among consumers with monthly consumption of more than 100 cubic meters. Consumers were given advice, as well as the necessary devices, to reduce consumption. Three months after the campaign started, average monthly water use had decreased another 29 percent.
- In its efforts to cut water use per capita by one-sixth, Mexico City has replaced 350,000 toilets with smaller six-liter models. This has saved enough water to meet the household needs of 250,000 residents.
- A new pricing system in Beijing links charges to the amount of water used. New administrative regulations set quotas on consumption and authorize fines for excessive use.
- The use of water-saving devices, leak detection and repair, and more efficient irrigation in its parks helped Jerusalem reduce its use of water per capita by 14 percent from 1989 to 1991.
- A water conservation program in Waterloo, Canada, included higher prices, education, and the distribution of water-saving devices. Volunteers distributed water conservation kits to nearly 50,000 homes. Water use per capita declined nearly 10 percent.

ing, restrictions on certain uses of water, programs that reduce leaks in water distribution systems, and educational programs that promote conservation. These measures, combined with economic incentives, have proved to be effective in times of water scarcity.

Decentralization, privatization, and user participation

Although the comprehensive analytical approach provides a framework for managing water resources, it does not require a centralized delivery of services. On the contrary, where local management capacities make it feasible, increasing the reliance on decentralized mechanisms changes the nature of the government's job.[5] Instead of distributing water, the central government should focus on establishing incentives to ensure that water is distributed in the desired quality and at the lowest possible price that reflects its value (taking into account the special needs of the poor).

DECENTRALIZATION. Water's special features make it difficult to rely exclusively on market forces to perform this function. For retail distribution, for example, the high fixed costs of piping systems for connecting households impart a tendency toward natural monopoly; hence, prices, if left to themselves, may be too high. If private firms are to be relied on, regulations governing pricing or mechanisms for ensuring competitive pressures are warranted, as are mechanisms to protect aquatic ecosystems. If public entities are to be relied on, experience suggests that financial autonomy and public participation are essential. In fact, programs that transfer existing government-managed water systems to private firms, financially autonomous utilities, and water user associations are being implemented in Latin America (Argentina, Colombia, and Mexico); Asia (Bangladesh, Indonesia, Nepal, Pakistan, Philippines, and Sri Lanka); Africa (Côte d'Ivoire, Madagascar, Morocco, Niger, Senegal, and Tunisia); and Eastern Europe (Hungary). In some countries, including Indonesia, Nepal, Netherlands, and Sri Lanka, the tradition of farmer-managed water service systems is centuries old. Early indications from recent country experiences suggest that there is indeed scope for achieving more efficient patterns of water use through reliance on decentralized mechanisms to deliver services.

ACCOUNTABILITY AND COST RECOVERY. Setting prices at the right level is not enough; prices need to be paid if they are to enhance the efficient allocation of resources. The record of nonpayment and noncollection of fees for water is long and well documented. It reflects two problems: weak incentives to collect and limited willingness to pay because services are poor. In many cases, the record of noncollections can be attributed to the lack of political determination to enforce collections and the limited motivation of agencies to collect, since they are not required to cover their costs. Not only have water charges been neglected, but so has cost recovery for services such as flood control, drainage, and sewage treatment. Failure to recover costs and reinvest in the systems leads to a vicious cycle whereby service declines with collections—as spare parts and essential materials run out—and consumers, in turn, become less willing to pay for the poor-quality services provided. Conversely, high collection rates often reflect decentralized management and enforced financial autonomy and accountability of water entities, which in turn deliver high-quality services for which consumers are willing to pay. Guinea provides a striking example of the scope that exists for rapidly breaking a vicious cycle by reorganizing the sector. Eighteen months after responsibility for supplying urban areas with water was turned over to a private supplier, the collection rate had improved from 15 to 70 percent, and service had likewise improved markedly.

FINANCIAL AUTONOMY. The lessons of experience suggest that an important principle in restructuring public service agencies is their conversion into financially autonomous entities, with effective authority to charge and collect fees and with freedom to manage without political interference. Such entities need to work under a hard budget constraint that enhances incentives for efficiency and revenue generation. Of greatest importance, the hard budget constraint unlocks incentives to collect fees and to provide services that consumers and farmers want. In the context of pricing that covers costs, the metering of water for urban, industrial, and agricultural users—and the ability to measure how much water individuals or firms receive and to charge them accordingly—opens the way for financial autonomy, accountability, and political independence of the water entities serving these users.

USER PARTICIPATION. The participation of users in managing and maintaining water facilities and operations brings many benefits. Participation in planning, operating, and maintaining irrigation works and facilities to supply water and sanitation services increases the likelihood that these will be well maintained and contributes to community cohesion and empowerment in ways that can spread to other development activities. This justifies the need to consistently promote the organization and strengthening of water user associations as a means to enhance participation and effectiveness in water management. In addition, governments benefit directly, as shown in a recent review of Bank-supported operations; financial and management burdens on government that result from administering water allocation can be reduced through user participation in both urban and rural areas (World Bank 1993b). Depending on the social context and local conditions, such participation can progressively increase in intensity over the project cycle, from consultation at the design stage to the actual operation and management of some parts of the system. In projects in Bangladesh and Kenya, users not only participate in establishing rural water and sanitation systems but also operate and manage them (box 3-5).

Box 3-5. Participation of Women in Water Supply and Sanitation Projects

The recognition of the crucial role that women play in water management at the household level has recently led to projects such as those in Kenya and Bangladesh, summarized below, which demonstrate the merits of women's participation. Both projects recognized that women would not automatically become involved and that a determined effort was necessary to ensure their participation. The projects emphasized community participation and included primary roles for women, but not to the exclusion of men.

In the southern coastal area of Kenya, a project to develop and install a system for hand pumps was begun in 1983. Early problems prompted the organizers to bring in a local NGO specializing in developing self-help water systems and focusing on women's participation. Women were trained as extension workers and in community organizing and development. Both men and women were trained for the appropriate maintenance and repairs. The local NGO motivated village men and women to organize themselves into water committees, which would be responsible for maintenance and repairs. By 1988, 135 village water committees were established, all of which had women as treasurers. All of the pumps were functioning. Both men and women had gained greater self-confidence and had an increased respect for, and acceptance of, women in public decisionmaking. Between 1985 and 1987, diarrhea declined 50 percent and a skin diseases 70 percent in the project area. The project also resulted in savings for both government and the villages.

In Mirzapur, Bangladesh, a program was created to install hand pumps and latrines. Again, the project was designed to be community based, with a strong emphasis on the inclusion of women. Women were involved from the beginning in selecting sites for hand pumps and latrines. They helped to cure the cement for the platforms and were trained to maintain both the pumps and the latrines. Women were also the main focus of the hygiene education program. In the intervention area, 148 hand pumps were installed (one for every thirty-three inhabitants) and 754 latrines. Most (90 percent) of the households used the hand pump for practically all domestic use compared with only 20 percent outside the intervention area. Virtually all (98 percent) of the adult population said they used the latrines regularly. Within the intervention area, there was a noticeable decline in diarrhea and other diseases. Essential to all of this was the strong participation of women.

WOMEN AND WATER. These projects in Bangladesh and Kenya highlight the importance of involving women, who essentially manage water at the household level, in the management of water systems. User studies show that women may, in arid environments or during dry periods in other climatic situations, spend up to eight hours a day collecting water. In many other cases, women spend 15 percent of their time fetching water. Given women's heavy work load, the time spent hauling water keeps them from other productive and household-caring activities and impairs their health and well-being. In urban areas, user participation that includes women is also promising for improving sanitation. In contrast to sewage treatment, which has strong public good characteristics, wastewater and solid waste collection tends to have more private good characteristics. Since many of the benefits from waste collection accrue to individual households, direct charges to the user should be an important source of financing. Nevertheless, community management can help bring costs down to affordable levels.

WATER USER ASSOCIATIONS. In irrigation projects, user participation helps promote sustainability by ensuring that design choices and operational practices are consistent with local crop requirements and farmer capacities. Such projects are more likely to be valued and maintained by the local population than projects without these elements (appendix C).[6] Governments are finding that by involving strong water user associations in project management and fee collection at the local level, they can use the capacity of community members to exert social pressure on their neighbors to pay. Equally, because association-managed systems have a consumer orientation, they are likely to provide better services and improve willingness to pay. There are early signs of significant progress in using water user associations, especially in small- and medium-size systems. Even large associations, such as those in Mendoza, Argentina, and Coello, Colombia, have proved effective. Governments can play an important role in fostering user participation by providing technical training for water user associations and community or institutional organizers (who have been very important in helping establish such associations in the Philippines and Sri Lanka). Local nongovernmental organizations (NGOs) can also help organize water users, as shown in Kenya (box 3-5).

PRIVATE SECTOR PARTICIPATION. Until relatively recently, private sector participation in the water supply sector was limited.[7] However, in the past few years, interest in private sector participation has burgeoned, and various innovative forms have emerged.[8] The most common form consists of concessions secured through competitive bidding. Typically, facilities are leased to the private operator, who contributes investment capital and who operates and maintains the facilities for a period of twenty to thirty years. Such arrangements are common in Côte d'Ivoire, France, Guinea, Macao, Portugal, and Spain and have been recently adopted in Argentina. Many countries in Eastern Europe and Latin America are contemplating similar approaches. Early in Chile's reform of water service delivery, the public water company in Santiago began using private contractors to read meters, maintain pipes, and handle billing. This raised staff productivity to the highest level among water and sanitation companies in Latin America. For sewerage systems—even in countries with a long history of private sector participation as, for example, in France—concession contracts are relatively rare. The predominant form of private involvement in sewerage systems is public investment coupled with a private management contract, typically for ten years. In irrigation, private sector participation has had notable successes in the sale, operation, and maintenance of tubewells, especially in Bangladesh, India, and Pakistan (appendix C).

FINANCING. Until now, the public sector has been the primary source of investment capital for the water sector. But, during the next ten years, the financial requirements for investments in irrigation, hydropower, and water supply and sanitation in developing countries are likely to be around $600 billion to $700 billion. New sources of capital will be needed, and the Bank will closely coordinate the activities it supports with other international and bilateral development agencies to help meet those needs through cofinancing and other mechanisms. The mix between private and public capital for investments in water resources will need to change, with the private sector share increasing sharply. The move toward greater reliance on financially autonomous entities, private firms, and water user organizations should open up new sources of private capital. Some of the autonomous entities and holders of operator contracts, once they prove to be financially viable, will be able to borrow through local and international capital markets, and scope will exist for support from the International Finance Corporation. The availability of private capital will depend to an important extent on the general development of the local capital market. The Bank's general effort to promote development of the financial sector is thus important in increasing the share of nongovernment financing of investment in water infrastructure. Water user associations should be able to obtain some investment funds from their members (in addition to achieving much higher levels of cost recovery than government agencies have). Thus, a mix of user charges, beneficiary taxes, central government transfers (grants and loans), and municipal and utility bonds will be required to meet future demand for investment.

Health and Environmental Resources

As demonstrated at the 1992 Earth Summit, governments increasingly recognize that more attention must be given to protect the quality of water and related environmental resources to ensure sustainable development and promote human health. To accomplish this, a balanced set of policies and institutions is needed that will take advantage of the efficiency provided by market forces while strengthening essential government policies and institutions targeted at environmental protection.

Improving municipal and industrial pollution abatement

Reducing water pollution in urban areas requires coordinated policies and steps to lower municipal and industrial discharges of wastewater. To reduce the cost of waste treatment, both industries and municipalities should be given incentives to reduce their waste loads based on the principle that the polluter pays. Municipal sewer and sewage treatment surcharges can be applied to water supply fees, preferably on the basis of volume. The industrial use of municipal sewerage systems should be based on clearly established standards for pretreatment and on user charges based on the volume and pollution load of industrial effluents. The Bank is developing best-practice guidelines for minimum levels of pollution control for both municipal and industrial sources. Establishing the appropriate standards requires careful analysis of the costs and benefits, given the very large price tag associated with cleanup operations and monitoring of enforcement. The cost of sewage treatment can be reduced by using innovative systems (for example, constructed wetlands), water conservation and demand management, isolation of toxic pollutants, and reuse for irrigation water.

EFFICIENCY IN ABATEMENT. Greater reliance on the private sector and financially autonomous utilities promises to lower costs and improve the management of sewerage systems. Such changes in management, combined with pricing policies to recover costs and other market-like approaches, including marketable pollution discharge permits, would improve wastewater treatment and generate sufficient funds for urban sanitation infrastructure. In smaller towns, villages, and rural areas, community-based water and waste disposal systems are likely to be most cost-effective, with governments helping to organize users and to establish a legal basis for communities to organize and charge users. To be effective, these systems should be based on community participation, with special emphasis on the participation of women.

DISCLOSURE OF EFFLUENT DISCHARGE DATA. Community participation can enhance official enforcement. A recent study in Bangladesh found that downstream villages pressured upstream polluters to install first-stage effluent treatment systems. With better information and legal support, such local participation could provide a cost-effective way to identify enforcement problems. The key is the public disclosure of information on the discharge of industrial and municipal pollution. Disclosure improves compliance by supplementing the limited monitoring resources of public agencies with the vigilance of affected communities. It strengthens enforcement efforts by focusing the attention of public officials on health and environmental problems associated with noncompliance.

Strengthening policies on land use and management

Integrating land use policies and practices with water management in river basins is important for formulating national strategies to manage water resources. The proper management of upstream watersheds is often critical for sustaining water projects, water quality, and aquatic ecosystems, which in turn helps sustain biodiversity. Incentives and programs are needed to improve land management practices in watersheds and to restore, then protect, environmental resources in floodplains and wetlands. Governments should intensify efforts to achieve flood control with nonstructural measures that are less costly, yet no less effective in preventing these disasters, than more expensive structural measures. These include a combination of market incentives and regulatory policies to reduce pollution, soil erosion, waterlogging, and flood runoff. The aim is to require land users to bear the costs that their land management practices impose on others and to encourage—through technical assistance, market incentives, and educational programs—cost-effective management practices that control surface and groundwater pollution and foster soil conservation.

CHANGING GOVERNMENT POLICIES. Government subsidies that induce activities harmful to the environment or that encourage wasteful use of water should be eliminated, and mining activities that seriously damage water resources should be regulated and controlled. In addition, when countries increase input levels to meet the growing demand for food, special measures, such as integrated pest management and the protection of groundwater recharge areas, should be implemented to prevent water contamination from agricultural chemicals.

GROUNDWATER PROTECTION. Groundwater is becoming increasingly important in water management and development, particularly in arid and semiarid regions. Its management should be integrated with surface water management in river basin systems. Emphasis should be placed

on land-based programs that use cost-effective best-management practices to protect the quality of groundwater in vulnerable geological areas,
in well fields, and in recharge areas. Measures should be taken to prevent
overpumping of coastal aquifers and aquifers underlain by saline aquifers, because excessive withdrawals can cause irreversible salt water
contamination. To restore polluted groundwater and to prevent further
contamination, appropriate environmental standards and codes of practice for safe transport, transfer, storage, and disposal of hazardous and
toxic wastes should be established and implemented. Drought planning
is also essential. Depletion of many aquifers should be reversed so that
emergency water can be stored and used to ensure the survival of
humans and the ecosystem during dry years.

Protecting environmental resources and social values during development

Environmental considerations need to be built into water projects. For
water investments, consideration should be given to protecting natural
ecosystems and to directing development to less sensitive or already
altered watersheds. Often, the best option may be to invest in existing
systems—to improve the controllability, adequacy, and reliability of
service—rather than in new systems. Where rehabilitation projects have
high rates of return, they should be given high priority. Moreover, using
regional environmental assessments early in the project cycle and ensuring that citizens, stakeholders, local NGOs, and disadvantaged groups
participate actively in the process should help define measures to reduce
a project's adverse impact on the ecosystem, avoid conflicts, minimize
confrontation, generate creative alternatives, and promote the sustainable development of water resources. Regional environmental assessments should be designed in the context of strategies for developing
river basin and regional development strategies. Upstream and downstream environmental impacts, including cumulative impacts, should
be examined and options for reducing negative, and for enhancing
positive, impacts should be considered. This examination should be
based on a careful collection, analysis, and public review of environmental information. Ecologically sustainable management, protection, and
restoration of groundwater recharge areas and water-dependent ecosystems also require the active involvement of the concerned populations
in managing and investing in the local resources. This, in turn, requires
certain and predictable land tenure. Thus, in water resource activities,
countries need to review the land tenure system and make the changes
necessary to give users adequate certainty regarding future land use.

RESETTLEMENT, INDIGENOUS PEOPLE, AND CULTURAL PROPERTY. Bank operational directives (appendix D) provide guidance on treating involuntary resettlement, indigenous people, and cultural property in the context of Bank-supported operations. However, they are also relevant for wider programs of public investment. Public sector water investments should ensure that adversely affected people, especially indigenous people, receive culturally acceptable social and economic benefits as well as access to water as part of any allocation process in a river basin. Resettlement should be avoided or minimized; if it is necessary, former incomes and living standards should be restored or improved. All the associated costs of doing so should be built into the investment costs of the project causing the displacement. Cultural heritage and equity considerations should be taken into account early in the process of project development. Hydrological architecture and traditional water structures of significance to affected peoples, as voiced during the environmental assessment process, should be recognized. Women's traditional role in securing water—and their potential role in educational training and informed participation in planning development projects—warrants special attention.

International Water Resources

Cooperation in managing the quality and quantity of water in international watercourses can benefit all the nations involved. Outside help can sometimes facilitate the negotiation of international agreements. For example, this was the case for two agreements recently signed between African countries: between Lesotho and South Africa for the Orange River and between Swaziland and South Africa for the Komati Basin with the concurrence of Mozambique, the third riparian country in the Komati.

International agreements

Overcoming institutional barriers to the management of international watercourses is not easy. Managing institutions, such as commissions or authorities, often involve only federal or central authorities, while state or provincial and local jurisdictions may have more responsibility for implementation. These barriers can be overcome through the involvement of all relevant jurisdictions, interagency cooperation, public participation, and fact-finding based on data sharing. Commissions or other managing entities should be positioned outside the direct control of individual governments and should remain impartial to preserve their independence as facilitators and independent evaluators. This concept is similar to that of separating operational from regulatory responsibility. Specific treaties or agreements are needed to codify the responsibilities of participating nations and the facilitating agency. A secretariat that reports to the entity or commission—not the government—is essential. (Appendix B gives an example of such an arrangement between the United States and Canada.)

Role for international organizations

The lessons of experience with agreements and joint actions between riparians, such as the Bank's difficult but successful nine-year effort to facilitate the 1960 Indus Water Treaty between India and Pakistan, suggest that external assistance and encouragement are valuable and sometimes essential ingredients in establishing international water agreements. Where the basic institutional framework exists, international agencies should provide support and encouragement. International agencies can also assist riparians in developing and managing water resources and in facilitating the implementation of treaties. The three main objectives of international efforts should be (a) to help riparian countries address problems with international water resources, (b) to unblock priority development activities that are held hostage by disputes over shared watercourses, and (c) to reduce inefficiencies in the use and development of scarce water resources caused by the lack of cooperative planning and development. Since no single international organization commands all the skills, experience, or resources necessary to achieve the needed cooperation, collaborative efforts among potential donors, international organizations, and NGOs would promote the sound management of international waters.

Notes

1. For small projects, the participation of beneficiaries is essential for the design and implementation to be effective. For very large water investments, governments should work toward establishing a national consensus on the desirability of moving ahead. Participation cannot be limited to the direct beneficiaries and those adversely affected. Persons and groups concerned about environmental consequences and secondary economic effects—especially for members of disadvantaged groups—need to be part of the decisionmaking process. Seeking broad participation will likely slow the approval process but will minimize delays in implementation that might occur if some persons feel they have not been consulted.

2. Provided that construction and management of the project do not harm the environment, hydropower can be a clean source of electricity. This, combined

with the rising cost of alternative sources of electric power, has favored the development of numerous hydropower projects in a number of developing countries. For example, almost 50 percent of Pakistan's and more than 26 percent of India's total generated energy come from hydropower. Thus, hydropower will continue to be a significant part of water and energy investments in some countries. For this to be done efficiently, investments in hydropower must be made in the context of overall national strategies for managing water and energy.

3. Compatible prices must reflect differences in delivery costs, location, time of year, quality, reliability, and policy distortions.

4. Per hectare charges also allow recovery of costs associated with other water services such as flood control and drainage.

5. Appendix A classifies water resource activities according to their market characteristics and indicates which services are best privatized. Appendix C provides examples of decentralized entities, including private firms and water user associations that provide and manage water resources. The various factors that make these entities successful are also spelled out.

6. Cernea (1992) and Bhatnagar and Williams (1992) provide a detailed discussion of building blocks for participation and of the Bank's experience in supporting the participatory approach to meeting development objectives. The Bank also established a Participatory Learning Group in 1991 with the financial support of the Swedish International Development Authority. The group is exploring opportunities for strengthening the Bank's support of popular participation in its development efforts.

7. Private ownership of water systems remains rare. Given the high fixed costs associated with water piping systems, such private companies tend to have natural monopoly positions. Suitable regulations are necessary to ensure that prices and investments are appropriate (appendix A).

8. The extreme occurred in England and Wales in 1990, when the government water entities were sold to the public and their shares were traded on the stock exchange.

4

The Role of the World Bank

The Bank will support national and international initiatives of member governments and international initiatives in implementing the approach described in chapter 3. It will focus its efforts on countries where significant problems exist or are emerging involving water scarcity, service efficiency, water allocation, or environmental damage. Its economic and sector work, lending, technical assistance, and participation in international initiatives will aim to promote policy and regulatory reforms; institutional adaptation and capacity building; environmental protection and restoration; and, when requested, cooperation in managing shared international watercourses. Because of the interdependencies among sectors, the impact of various economic activities on water resources, and the important social aspects of water allocation and services, the Bank will incorporate issues of water resource policy and management in its policy dialogue and country assistance strategies when such issues are significant. Because of the magnitude of the need that some countries have for investment and capacity building in water resources, the Bank will seek to coordinate its activities with international and bilateral agencies providing similar types of assistance. In many circumstances, cofinancing will be useful and feasible, while in other cases, establishing a division of labor among donors according to their comparative advantages will improve the effectiveness of development efforts.

Experience with Water Resource Management

Investments in water resources have played a major role in the Bank's efforts to help countries reduce poverty and upgrade living conditions. Irrigation systems have expanded food production, improved nutrition, and increased rural incomes. Investments in water and sanitation systems also have improved health and living standards. Hydropower projects have been an important source of energy for industrial and agricultural development. By the end of 1991, more than $19 billion had been lent for irrigation and drainage, $12 billion for water supply and sewerage, and about $9 billion for hydropower projects, the total representing more than 15 percent of total Bank lending. This division into single-purpose projects for irrigation and drainage, water supply and sanitation, and hydropower generation reflects the institutional structure found in most countries, where specialized government agencies are responsible for such individual subsectors.

Subsector strategies

Bank assistance has evolved from simple project lending toward country-focused support for elaborating and implementing subsectoral strategies. These strategies are developed through sector work and subsectoral reviews in which priorities are articulated and performance is analyzed. The growing involvement in subsector strategies has included giving greater attention to policy issues such as pricing and decentralization that extend beyond the context of the individual projects. Institutional development and capacity building have also increasingly been addressed in Bank-supported projects, in contrast to the Bank's earlier focus mostly on hardware. More recently, the increased pressure on limited water resources in many member countries has caused a reassessment of the narrow subsectoral perspective. Thus, the Bank has started to consider cross-sectoral issues in the context of water operations and the assessment of national strategies for managing water resources.

Implementation of Bank policies

The Bank's operational policies and procedures provide the basis for investments in water resources designed to make operations efficient, equitable, transparent, and environmentally sound. But as operational reviews, Operations Evaluation Department (OED) evaluations, and other studies point out, the Bank has not always strictly implemented these policies (World Bank 1990a; 1990b, chap. 10; 1993b; and box 4-1). The problems identified include failure to address water resource issues in a comprehensive manner; improper attention to financial covenants and inadequate cost recovery; lack of accountability, autonomy, and flexibility in water management; inadequate investment in sewage treatment and in drainage systems; inadequate concern for poverty relief;

Box 4-1. Project Ratings of the Bank's Operations Evaluation Department

In its 1988 review of approximately 234 water projects for 1974–88, the Bank's Operations Evaluation Department (OED) found that 88 percent of the investments in water supply and sanitation and 80 percent of those in irrigation were satisfactory. This compares with 81 percent for all Bank projects reviewed. In general, these projects have provided potable water and hydroelectric power for some of the world's poorest cities and irrigation water to improve food security and farm family incomes. In addition, many projects judged to be unsatisfactory have provided substantial benefits.

However, project ratings have dropped sharply for the projects completed in recent years. The percentage of irrigation projects rated satisfactory dropped to 44 percent during 1989–90 before rising to 71 percent in 1991, while a decline also occurred in water supply and sanitation projects during 1990–91 (56 percent were satisfactory). It is not clear how much of the drop reflects a real decline in performance and how much reflects a more realistic evaluation of the weaknesses associated with many water projects. The original performance ratings were based on a single criterion, while the more recent ratings were based on a broader assessment. The weaknesses pointed out by OED reports have been exacerbated by the increasing complexity of more recent projects developed to meet the rapidly growing demand for reliable and good-quality water supplies.

---

neglect of operations and maintenance; delayed and poor-quality construction; lack of consideration of environmental assessments and pollution control; inadequate concern for project sustainability; and lack of programs to address erosion problems in upstream watersheds (appendix E). Many of the problems reflect the lack of incentives facing government entities providing water services and the consumers' lack of willingness to pay water charges. The lessons learned from Bank experience are already being incorporated in new projects supported by the Bank, which rely more heavily on participatory approaches, private sector involvement, and comprehensive management (box 4-2). The new policy promoted in this paper reflects many of the insights gained.

Areas of Involvement

The analysis in chapter 2 pointed out the prevalence of market failures in managing water resources and highlighted weaknesses in past

Box 4-2. Innovative Features of Recent Bank-Sponsored Water Resource Activities

The Bank, through its lending programs, encourages borrowers to implement new approaches to meet the continuing challenges of water resource development. The following are recent examples of innovative Bank-supported approaches to managing water resources.

- Pakistan's Rural Water Supply and Sanitation Project is developing a delivery mechanism whereby rural communities would provide, operate, and maintain, to the extent possible, the service for themselves.
- Recognizing the need to incorporate users in operations and maintenance, Indonesia is transferring irrigation systems of 500 hectares and less to water user groups.
- In Nepal much of the new investment in irrigation is driven by demand. Legal farmer associations request investment and agree to contribute some capital costs and take responsibility for operations and maintenance upon completion.
- Mexico is in the process of transferring seventy-eight irrigation districts (covering more than 1.8 million hectares) to water user associations. These groups will be responsible for operating and maintaining all canals and water distribution.
- An enabling environment was established in Bangladesh that allowed the private sector to take responsibility for selling and maintaining low-lift pumps and shallow tubewells. The number of tubewells in use has grown substantially, with a subsequent increase in market activity for water.
- In Cyprus's southeast coast, treated wastewater will be distributed from a main trunk line to irrigate public parks and tourist areas. Sewage disposal needs will be met while supporting the development of the coastal tourist industry.

governments' approaches to deal with these failures. The key weaknesses involving government actions include (a) fragmented government decisionmaking regarding water resources, which leads to unsound regulations, environmental policies, water allocation, and public investment choices; (b) excessive reliance on overextended government agencies to the neglect of private firms, autonomous utilities operating under the discipline of financial accountability, and community organizations; and (c) neglect of the environmental and health consequences of public sector policies and investments. These are at the

- Under provisions of a 1986 treaty, the Lesotho Highlands Water Authority will export water to South Africa. South Africa will ultimately meet all costs of the transfer. Revenues from this project are projected to equal 25 percent of Lesotho's exports until 2045.
- In its Water Sector Modernization Project, Brazil is establishing an independent regulatory framework and helping state water companies to attain financial self-sufficiency and corporate autonomy.
- In Maharastra, India, rural water will be supplied from village piped water systems and individual hand pumps. The sanitation component will promote the disposal of wastewater through improved drainage and the construction of low-cost latrines. The project will also strengthen the system for monitoring water quality throughout the state.
- In order to rehabilitate the technical, commercial, and financial operations of the water supply sector in Guinea, a project supports a water management company, jointly owned by the state and a foreign investor/manager, with a lease contract to supply Conakry with water.
- Until Cyprus implemented a comprehensive water plan, the island was depleting its groundwater. Under this plan, various catchment and conveyance structures were constructed, and water was allocated to two municipalities and three irrigation areas. The project was executed by the Ministry of Agriculture and Natural Resources and offered agricultural services such as a user-controlled water distribution system, operations and maintenance equipment, a research station, and roads.
- In three Brazilian states, water quality and pollution control projects emphasize basin management by creating basin authorities and institutional, legal, and regulatory frameworks that facilitate cross-sectoral and cross-governmental coordination while delegating many responsibilities to municipalities.

root of many of the difficulties encountered by Bank-supported projects in the past. National policy reforms to be supported by the Bank are designed to redress these past weaknesses and, in turn, to improve the delivery of services. As outlined in chapter 3, the approach involves the development of a country-specific national strategy for water resources management. While promoting institutional change to increase the coordination among water entities and agencies, implementation of this strategy will entail greater reliance on decentralized units, community water management, and pricing (and markets where they can be established) to provide incentives for efficient and sustainable delivery of water services. Such an approach would preserve scarce government implementation capacity for tasks that would not otherwise be performed. Accordingly, the Bank will support greater use and enforcement of pricing and cost recovery to motivate efficient delivery of services and use of water. It will also support policy reforms designed to protect the environment more effectively.

Comprehensive framework

Giving priority to countries with significant water management problems, the Bank will encourage and assist countries in the development of a systematic framework for incorporating cross-sectoral and ecosystem interdependencies into the formulation of policies, regulations, and public investment plans that are suitable to the particular country's situation. The framework will foster transparent decisions and emphasize demand management. It will be designed so that the options for public water management in a river basin or watershed can be evaluated and compared within a national water strategy and the various economic, social, and environmental objectives that countries adopt. It will also enable coherent public investment plans to be formulated at the national and basin level and consistent policies and regulations to be developed across sectors. This will allow simplification of individual projects, thus enhancing their likelihood of success. To facilitate the introduction of such a framework, the Bank is ready to support capacity building by enhancing analytical capabilities, adopting participatory techniques, and strengthening data bases, as well as by conducting water resource assessments and related institutional changes.

In its operations, the Bank will promote the creation and strengthening of hydrologic, hydrogeologic, water quality, and environmental data bases for both surface and groundwater. It will encourage the development and use of adequate data bases regarding the various elements of the water system. This information will be an important input into a country's national water strategy and environmental action plan. To facilitate the collection of data, the Bank will support the use of modern technologies for hydrologic and environmental monitoring and for surveys and data processing, taking into account the relation between the costs and benefits of more detailed information. Since improved information systems are a key input for comprehensive water management, the Bank will help countries to develop systems that effectively use the data to monitor current changes in water supply and demand, thereby improving decisionmaking.

Institutional and regulatory systems

The reform of water resource management policies will have implications for the institutions dealing with water resources. Where appropriate and feasible, the Bank will help governments to reform and establish a strong legal and regulatory framework to tackle social concerns, monopoly pricing, and environmental protection. Similarly, the Bank will support the adaptation of institutional structures at the national and regional levels to coordinate the formulation and implementation of policies for improved water management and public investment programs. In many countries, institutional reform will focus on river basins as the appropriate unit for analysis and coordinated management. Also, where appropriate, the Bank will promote river basins as an effective way to integrate and monitor activities concerning land use, availability and quality of water, conjunctive use of surface and groundwater resources, biodiversity, floodplain and drought risk management, and protection of river basin environments. Such coordinating arrangements are particularly important in countries with federal structures, in which provincial or state governments have complete authority over the management of water resources in their jurisdiction. Before committing funds to support operations with important interstate effects, the Bank will require legislation, or other appropriate arrangements, establishing effective coordination and agreed procedures for allocating water among states. Furthermore, the Bank will use water resource sector loans to facilitate efforts to coordinate activities across sectors.

In tandem with promoting a comprehensive framework and with institutional and policy reforms, policy analysts, planners, managers, and technicians in the country will have to upgrade their skills. Accordingly, the Bank will support training in cross-sectoral analysis; legal, regulatory, and privatization issues; and river basin management, environmental protection, project formulation and evaluation, demand forecasting, and participatory management. This is an immense task that can be accomplished only in stages. The Economic Development Institute of the World Bank will be an important element in this training effort, through a special initiative that supports the implementation of the new policy.

Incentives

Many of the problems encountered in providing water services are due to the lack of incentives both for performance by providers and for efficiency by users. Thus, a key component of the reforms to be supported by the Bank will be greater reliance on incentives for efficiency and financial discipline. The Bank will highlight the importance of pricing and financial accountability. In principle, this entails the use of water fees to broadly reflect the opportunity cost of water. However, given the presently low level of cost recovery and the political difficulty involved in the immediate adoption of opportunity cost pricing, a good starting point is pricing to ensure financial autonomy. Since in most cases, these prices will not assure optimal allocation of water resources, other mechanisms such as water trading, administrative reallocation, and other demand management strategies will be needed.

POVERTY ALLEVIATION. Inadequate water services have a particularly adverse impact on the poor, facilitating the spread of disease, especially in crowded, low-income areas. Thus, special efforts should be directed to meeting the water needs of the poor and to redressing the neglect of the rural poor as spelled out in the *Poverty Reduction Handbook* (World Bank 1992c). Furthermore, better hygiene should be emphasized so that the health benefits from improved water supply are fully realized. Where public finance is scarce, significant additional resources can often be mobilized within local communities. Attention should be paid to ascertaining from the poor the level of services they want and to providing a range of service levels. Where the poor are unable to pay for an acceptable level of services, "social fees," whereby the better-off cross-subsidize the poor, and budgetary transfers, which subsidize connections, can be used. Caution is required so as not to jeopardize the financial viability and autonomy of water entities. Policies that affect or change water rights should be carefully evaluated to ensure that they do not harm the poor, since water rights are often crucial for generating income. Where necessary, adjustments should be accompanied by compensatory measures.

DECENTRALIZATION. Because their financial and administrative resources are limited, governments need to be selective in the responsibilities they assume for water resources. Where local and private capabilities are adequate and where appropriate regulatory and environmental protection systems are in place, the Bank will support efforts of central governments to decentralize responsibilities to local governments and to transfer service delivery functions to the private sector, to financially autonomous public corporations, and to community organizations such as water user associations. Arrangements for performance accountability will be incorporated into Bank-supported activities. The privatization of public water service agencies or their transformation into financially autonomous entities and the use of management contracts for service delivery will be encouraged. These steps will improve incentives for recovering costs and providing better services and will give users a sense of ownership and participation. In countries where provincial and municipal skills are inadequate to manage complex water resource systems, the Bank should support efforts to improve local management skills through training and capacity building programs so that decentralization can eventually be implemented. Pilot projects will help to introduce new forms of decentralized management and to refine the design to suit local circumstances.

PARTICIPATION. Participation empowers stakeholders to influence the formulation of policy, the choice of design and investment, and management decisions affecting their communities; it also establishes the necessary sense of ownership. As discussed in chapter 3, as participation increases, service delivery and cost recovery will likely improve. Therefore, the Bank will encourage the participation of beneficiaries and affected parties in the design and implementation of projects it supports. The Bank already requires consultation with affected people and local NGOs in the context of environmental assessments and will promote the participation of concerned people—including the poor, indigenous people, and disadvantaged groups—in the water-related operations it supports. Particular attention will be given to the participation of women since they are essentially the managers of domestic water. The Bank will encourage governments to follow these principles more broadly in their investment programs and other activities related to water resources.

Health and environmental protection

The protection, enhancement, and restoration of water quality and the abatement of water pollution will be a focus of Bank-supported operations, particularly given the importance of providing safe drinking water, which is so critical for improving human health. Accordingly, the Bank will increase its support for government efforts to promote sanitation, wastewater collection and treatment, and, where possible, water reuse in various economic activities. The Bank will promote efforts to develop innovative technical, financial, and institutional approaches that reduce unit costs, foster water conservation, and ensure the efficient delivery and management of services. The Bank will support efforts to adapt and implement cost-effective technologies for improved water supplies, flood control, pollution monitoring and control, and low-cost treatment of waste. The Bank will promote research, development, and adaptation of technologies that modernize irrigation distribution systems and improve water use efficiency, sustainability, and operations and maintenance. To facilitate the introduction and adaptation of new technologies, the Bank will support the development and use of pilot programs and, once proven, their wider replication.

INDUSTRIAL AND URBAN POLLUTION. For industrial waste and mining discharges, the emphasis will be on establishing incentives, such as pollution charges based on the principle of the polluter pays, and effective government institutions and regulations to reduce effluents—especially toxic substances—at their source and to encourage reuse of wastewater. The Bank is preparing guidelines that outline best practices for abating industrial pollution and minimizing waste and will promote their use as part of its policy dialogue with countries. Public disclosure of information relating to industrial and municipal effluent or waste discharges helps communities to pursue and implement policies that protect public health and environmental sustainability. Accordingly, as part of the environmental assessment, the Bank requires public disclosure of such information in the activities it supports and will encourage national implementation as part of capacity building.

AGRICULTURAL AND RURAL POLLUTION. On pollution originating from agricultural activities, the Bank will support governmental actions to restore and protect surface and subsurface waters degraded by agricultural pollutants and to minimize soil erosion. Such actions will include implementing best management practices and pricing policies that incorporate environmental effects as well as making complementary investments in erosion control, reforestation, and watershed protection and restoration. The Bank will also pay special attention to the problems of waterlogging and salinity associated with irrigation investments. Provisions for implementing drainage networks, where necessary, will be incorporated and enforced by requiring that water tables be monitored in irrigation projects so that drainage works are established before problems emerge and that best management practices be installed to control water pollution.

ECOSYSTEMS. The Bank will offer its assistance to governments in developing strategies and cost-effective mechanisms for the ecologically sustainable management, protection, and restoration of recharge areas and water-dependent ecosystems, such as wetlands, riverine floodplain areas, estuaries, and coastal zones. Such systems serve as biophysical filters, safeguard biological diversity, and conserve water resources. Restoration of these ecosystems is an integral part of improving the management of water resources.

GROUNDWATER PROTECTION. Given the increasing importance of groundwater, especially in arid and semiarid areas, the Bank will pay attention to the linkages between ground and surface water in the management of river basins and will support the establishment of government programs and policies to restore and protect the quality of groundwater and to preserve groundwater recharge areas. In addition, where appropriate, the Bank will seek to reverse the depletion of groundwater and encourage the adoption of demand management and of water conservation practices so that withdrawals from aquifers remain sustainable.

Cooperative management of international water resources

Existing guidelines describe Bank policy on the financing of projects on international waterways (appendix D). The Bank will help countries improve their management of shared international water resources, for example, by supporting the analysis of development opportunities forgone because of international water disputes. Through technical, financial, and legal assistance, the Bank, if requested, will help governments establish or strengthen institutions, such as river basin organizations, to address transnational water management activities. Furthermore, the Bank will support studies and consultations to review available organizational arrangements and help develop alternative solutions. A flexible approach will be adopted in any initial contact with riparians, avoiding preconditions to the extent possible, in order to explore the most appropriate form of assistance that the Bank may offer. The Bank will be sensitive at all times to the interests of all riparian parties, as all parties must be treated even-handedly. The focus will be on international watercourses in which the Bank's assistance is likely to have a substantial impact.

GLOBAL ENVIRONMENT FACILITY. The incremental cost of actions taken by riparian states to protect international water resources and river basins will continue to be financed within the framework of the Global Environment Facility (GEF). Within activities related to the pollution of international waters (projected to be 10 to 20 percent of its budget during the pilot phase), the GEF will address problems in several shared marine and freshwater resources. For example, it is supporting three closely coordinated projects designed to provide a long-term solution to the pollution problems found in the Danube River Basin and related environmental impacts in the Black Sea.

GROUNDWATER. Transnational groundwater resources are not covered by the present Bank policy on transnational water resources. There is an ongoing effort by the International Law Commission to formulate rules for the use of international groundwater, and the Bank will monitor these efforts. Since some aspects of groundwater are not well understood, the Bank will promote the acquisition of knowledge concerning internationally shared groundwater to provide a basis for establishing guidelines governing the Bank's activities. The Bank, where appropriate, will promote the sustainable use of international groundwater.

Implications for Bank Operations

Countries differ in their water requirements and endowments, their poverty profiles, their institutional capacities, and the problems they face from environmental degradation. Thus, the specific design of relevant reforms, and the time frame for implementation, will need to be developed and evaluated case by case. Nonetheless, the introduction of the recommended reforms will typically entail difficult political choices and tradeoffs between conflicting objectives, such as financial viability and the needs of the poor, environmental sustainability and cost-effectiveness, and domestic water demands and expanded food production. Commitments by governments will therefore be essential to implement the necessary reforms. Furthermore, given the present status of water resource management and institutions in many countries, the implementation of the necessary changes will take time. Accordingly,

- In countries with significant problems of water resource management, the Bank will assist governments through sector work, technical assistance, and environmental action plans. In collaboration with other international and national agencies, it will help identify and formulate priority policy and institutional reforms and investments and determine their appropriate sequencing. These priorities—and the degree of government commitment to them—will be highlighted in the country assistance strategy and will guide the sectoral lending program.
- The priority reforms and activities to be addressed in analytical work at the national and basin level and referred to in the country assistance strategy will deal with issues such as (a) the appropriate incentive framework and pricing; (b) service delivery to the poor;

(c) public investment priorities; (d) environmental restoration and protection; (e) water resource assessment and data requirements; (f) comprehensive analytical framework; and (g) legislation, institutional structures, and capacities. Assessing the degree of government commitment to implementing the requisite reforms will be an important part of the analysis.

- Progress in implementing the priorities identified will be monitored through normal Bank interactions with the country. If the absence of adequate progress on priority actions is judged to produce serious misuse of resources and to hamper the viability of water-related investments, Bank lending in this area will be limited to the provision of potable water to poor households and to operations designed to conserve water and protect its quality without additionally drawing on a country's water resources. Such operations include sanitation, waste treatment, water reuse and recycling, abatement of water pollution, drainage, and rehabilitation of the distribution system. These investments will be assessed on their individual merits.
- Individual lending operations for water projects should discuss the linkage to priorities for reform, investment, and Bank support, as well as the likely impact of the overall water-related program. The analysis of operations will include an assessment of the implications for other sources of water, using subsectors within the relevant regional setting, most likely a river basin. Relevant pricing issues, the record on cost recovery, and financial autonomy and sustainability will receive particular attention. The rationale for institutional arrangements for implementation, particularly the division of responsibilities between government and nongovernmental or financially autonomous entities, will be provided. These issues will be discussed in the relevant project documents. The Bank requires assessment of the environmental impacts of projects, environmental assessments of the entire river basin for significant water-related projects, and full consultation with affected people and local organizations.

Procedures, Staffing, and Training

Many of the policies promoted in this paper, such as cost recovery, privatization, participatory approaches, and environmental protection, can be implemented through existing Bank procedures because they are consistent with operational guidelines already in effect (appendix D). In addition, the national environmental action plans being prepared by the Bank's borrowers can be used to identify priority areas for investments in improving the management of water resources and in protecting water-dependent ecosystems.

Organization

Other policies recommended in this paper require specific implementation procedures. Although Bank operations are typically handled within sectoral divisions, project designs need to consider cross-sectoral issues as well as cumulative impacts at the level of the region and the basin. Various arrangements are possible to ensure that the Bank's water-related activities for a country (or a group of countries in the case of international systems) are treated in a comprehensive manner. One example is to rely on the country team, in collaboration with the project adviser and lead economist, to ensure coordination. Some departments have established cross-sectoral water teams, and one vice presidency has a central water unit. In formulating the country assistance strategy, departments will judge the priority that should be given to water resource activities compared with the priority given to other sectors.

Implementation

To help implement this policy for managing water resources, the Bank will undertake a range of activities, including the preparation of guidelines and best-practices papers, staff and country training programs, capacity building, and the development of coordination mechanisms to improve water resources management. More specifically, in collaboration with the United Nations Development Programme, a guide on capacity building is being proposed for countries interested in formulating water resource management strategies. Guides are also being prepared on establishing water resource information systems, on best practices for setting up coordinating mechanisms, on generalized economic models for conducting river basin analysis, and on best management practices for water user associations. Regional units are preparing regional water strategies, which incorporate the recommendations of this water policy within the specific circumstances of their areas. An analysis of available and required Bank staff in the area of water resource management has been conducted, and training programs, workshops, and seminars are being prepared to upgrade staff skills. Pilot projects will be used to implement some of the newer aspects of the water policy such as decentralization and opportunity cost pricing. Finally, implementation of the new water policy will be reviewed in two years.

Skills mix

Implementing the policies outlined in this paper requires adjustments in the level of skill and mix of staff that can only be achieved progressively over time. Introducing the new policy will require more specialists. Staff will need training in methodologies for project appraisal and economic evaluation that incorporate multisectoral aspects and in participatory approaches to designing and implementing projects. The new aspects of water-related operations under this policy will require more staff time and will need to be reflected in the resources assigned to such operations. The qualitative and quantitative upgrading of specialized and other staff is essential to meet the difficult challenges of managing water resources in the coming century.

Appendix A. Market Failures and Public Policy in Water Management

Public finance theory and welfare economics provide the analytical framework for examining the public and private good characteristics of water resource activities as well as other attributes determining the efficiency of market forces.[1] The provision and some of the production of pure public goods are essentially the responsibility of the government, while pure private goods can be handled efficiently by markets. Most water activities, however, are not strictly public or private goods. Frequently they require some form of government regulation or involvement if the resources are to be used reasonably efficiently. This appendix provides information to support judgments about the relative roles that the public and private sector should play in specific activities.

Public Goods

The basic criteria for assessing the degree to which a good or a service is closer to being public than private pertain to subtractability and excludability. Subtractability occurs with most traditional goods, such as ice cream, where one person's use or consumption of the good or service decreases or subtracts from its value to others who use the same good or service (if one person eats the ice cream, another person cannot have it). For public goods, there is no conventional consumption during use (zero subtractability), and the goods can continue to provide the same benefits to everyone, as long as they are not damaged or congested (for example, navigation as long as there is no congestion). When use can be increased without any cost to society or subtraction from benefits to other consumers (the marginal cost of serving another user is zero), increased use adds to total economic welfare. Low subtractability characterizes facilities such as sewer and water lines and navigation channels as long as they are being used below full capacity.

A second characteristic of public goods is the inability to exclude, or the high cost of preventing a consumer, who does not meet the conditions set by the supplier, from using the resource. Many water-related activities are characterized by the difficulty of excluding people from their use (for example, large irrigation schemes based on gravity flow, where the monitoring of individual use is costly; village wells; and flood control). If a dam is built to provide flood control on a stream, no one along the stream can be excluded from receiving the benefits of flood control. This is quite different from a park, around which a fence can be erected and from which persons who do not pay the entrance fee can be excluded.

These two characteristics (subtractability and excludability) can be used to set up a broad two-way classification of goods and services: (a) public goods (low subtractability and excludability) include goods such as flood control and large multipurpose dams, (b) private goods (high subtractability and excludability) include goods such as ice cream and bread, (c) toll goods (low subtractability and high excludability) involve goods such as conventional sewerage systems and navigation facilities, and (d) open access goods (high subtractability and low excludability) include resources such as aquifers with low recharge rates and many ocean fisheries. Private firms do not engage in activities with low excludability, because it is difficult to get consumers to pay. Thus governments may have to provide funding to establish such activities. Where low excludability causes the resource to be overused, such as occurs with groundwater, government regulations may be necessary. Where low subtractability exists, market forces do not produce an optimal level of output, and government investments or subsidies may be required. If both characteristics (public goods) are present, then government investment is needed, but management may be contracted to the private sector or user groups.

Market Power

Market forces can generate an efficient (economic) allocation of resources when the market is competitive. However, economic activities in which there are economies of scale (a large fixed cost relative to variable costs) or economies of scope (lower unit costs of producing several products in combination rather than separately, such as multipurpose water projects) tend to become "natural" monopolies. In such a situation, the market is dominated by a single supplier. When the market is characterized by a monopoly, resource allocation is deficient, since monopolistic entities tend to produce less and charge more for any good or service than would be the case under competitive conditions. Furthermore, because the threat of entry by would-be competitors is minor, incentives for innovation and dynamic efficiency are diminished. Market forces thus do not bring about a desired resource allocation when a natural monopoly exists. Examples of natural monopolies are large dams, main canal networks, and large urban sewerage and water systems.

The extent of inefficiency in such a situation is determined by the perceived risk of potential entry of competitors, since this perception influences the behavior of the monopolistic entity. If large fixed costs need to be invested that cannot be recovered in the case of unsuccessful entry, the degree of contestability is limited, and the potential for inefficiency is high.[2] Many of the facilities for water-related activities require large fixed costs and are thus prone to the problems of natural monopolies. However, operating and maintaining these facilities, once they are built, may not require a high set-up cost (fixed cost). For example, systems that supply piped water entail expensive infrastructure, but their operation and maintenance do not and, therefore, could be handled by small private firms. These aspects are thus characterized by a high degree of contestability.

Externalities

Because water activities have many physical interactions within the ecosystem and with other economic activities, they are often characterized by externalities. That is, the benefits and costs of production and consumption affect individuals or entities other than those involved in a transaction. Negative externalities imply overproduction of the activity involved, while positive externalities imply underproduction. Examples of negative externalities include the contamination of surface and groundwater by sewage and chemicals and saline water from irrigation, degradation of wetlands due to the diversion of water resources, and the lowering of the water table (thus increasing the cost of pumping) by drawing on a common aquifer. An example of a positive externality is the health benefit to the general population of connecting individuals to a sewer system.

Related to the issue of externalities is the limited amount of information available to the consumers (and sometimes producers) of water services. The complexities of the ecosystem within which water is a component, the variability of the water supply, and the intricacies of the hydrological cycle make it difficult for those transacting with water to consider all aspects. Consequently, market prices do not necessarily reflect all these interrelations.

Merit Goods

Some water services cater to social objectives that have a wide political acceptance and are thus considered merit goods, that is, their consumption has a benefit to society beyond that which accrues to the individuals consuming them. The access to a certain minimum level of water for human consumption is generally perceived to be such a good, hence subsidies to enhance access to water supplies are common. Merit goods generally have extremely low price elasticities of demand at low (basic) levels of use (for example, the domestic consumption of water). Because some water services such as drinking water are merit goods, they receive political attention, and private entities providing these services can be subjected to political intervention, especially if prices are high. Furthermore, since water used in other activities (such as irrigation) could potentially be used for human consumption, entities dealing with such services could also be affected by government interventions.

Transaction Costs

The difficulty of establishing enduring and secure water rights has been an important factor in raising the cost that users pay for water transactions, particularly in the agricultural sector. In addition, the bulky nature of water generally requires expensive conveyance infrastructure to move significant quantities upstream or outside river basins, thus preventing the development of national water markets, except for bottled water. In many water systems based on gravity flow (as are many irrigation systems), water rights are defined by a share of flow in the canal or river. In such cases, transactions between individuals who are not adjacent to one another require changes in the physical apparatus controlling the intervening use of water or changes in the scheduling of flows. These changes have to be agreed to by all individuals affected, even those who are not parties in the transactions. If the transacting parties are located at different outlets of a canal, the cost of introducing the adjustments to all users affected can be high. Transactions between groups may require fewer physical adjustments or simpler scheduling revisions, but they typically entail the complexities of organizing for collective action. Thus there can be a high transaction cost to trading water among users, which tends to create fragmented markets.

Table A-1 characterizes various water activities according to the market failures affecting them. Technology, institutions, social norms, and the enforcement apparatus influence the classification of particular services, and, as these factors change over time, services may shift category.

Policy Implications

The range of market failures in the water management activities reviewed here justifies government actions or other forms of collective actions to ameliorate the inefficiencies likely to result without government action. In determining the role of government, it is useful to distinguish between the *provision* and the *production* of infrastructure. The provision of infrastructure involves the set of decisions and actions that enable infrastructure facilities and services to be made available. Examples are a legal framework that allows water user organizations to tax landowners and invest in irrigation systems or a direct government investment in the construction of a water supply system. Production is the act of executing investment and generating services, such as a private contractor building a dam or managing a government-owned sewerage plant. Provision and production need not necessarily be done by the same organization.

Analysis of specific water activities leads to the conclusion that the provision of network facilities, especially at the primary (or trunk) level, investment planning, and some technical assistance have a significant public good nature, and that the facilities are by and large natural monopolies (for example, piped water supply and sewerage, large-scale irrigation networks). However, the generation and maintenance of many of the services from these networks can often be implemented under conditions of excludability, and they can be subject to a degree of contestability. They can, therefore, be subjected to some competitive market forces (for example, by opening the market for a contract to operate and maintain a sewerage system for a specified time period to competing bids that may or may not be renewed). Furthermore, many of the externalities related to the extraction and use of water can be internalized through taxes and subsidies and, where effective monitoring is feasible, through the enforcement of regulations. Some of the impediments to the creation of markets or to the ability to conduct transactions in water can be ameliorated through the use of tradable water rights, institutional mechanisms to resolve conflicts over water use, and technologies that facilitate the monitoring of individual water use and enable conveyance between users. Because this can be expensive, the gains in efficiency need to be weighed against the costs of installing the new technology. Table A-2 describes the link between market failures and remedial policy in the water sector.

Table A-1. Characteristics of Public and Private Goods, Market Power, and Externalities in Water Sector Services

| | Nature of the good | | Market power, | | |
Type of system	Subtractability	Excludability	contestability	Externalities	Comment
Wastewater management					
Conventional sewerage					
Sreet sewer line	L	H	L	PH, WP	Toll goods
Pumping stations	L	H	L	PH, WP	Toll goods
Treatment plants	L	H	L	PH, WP	Toll goods
Intermediate- or low-cost sewerage					
Condominial sewerage	M	M	M	PH, WP	Public good characteristics
Localized treatment	M	M	M	PH, WP	Public good characteristics
Other intermediate sewerage	M	M	M	PH, WP	Public good characteristics
Basic sanitation (pit latrine)	H	M	H	PH, WP	Private good characteristics
Water supply					
Piped water					
Trunk system (intake pumping station)	H[a]	H	L	PH, GD	Private good characteristics
Distribution system	L	M	L	PH	Public good characteristics
Terminal equipment					
Common (hand pump)	M	L	H	PH	SF, public good characteristics
Individual (home faucet)	M	H	H	PH	Private good characteristics
Village wells	M	L	H	PH	SF, public good characteristics
Vending (tanker trunks)	H	H	H	PH	Private good

Irrigation

Surface water

Trunk system (dam, main canal)	M^b	M	L	WL, E	Public good characteristics
Distribution system (secondary and tertiary canal)	M^b	M	M	WL, ND	Public good characteristics
Terminal system (on farm), gravity					
Field-to-field irrigation	H	L	H^c	WL, ND, S	Open access resource
Individual farm	H	H	H^c	WL, ND, S	Private good, HTC
Terminal system requiring lift	H	H	H^c	WL, ND, S	Private good

Groundwater

Deep tubewells					
Pumping facilities using open access	H^a	H	M	GD	Private good using open access resource
Distribution system	M	M	M	WL, S	Public good characteristics
Terminal system	H	H	H^c	WL, S	Private good
Shallow tubewells	H^a	H	H	WL, S	Private good using open access resources

Run of the river systems

Headworks	M^b	M	M		Public good characteristics
Distribution system	M^b	M	M	WL, S	Public good characteristics
Terminal system	H	H	H^c	WL, S	Private good, HTC

Small dams and reservoirs

Headworks	M^b	M	M		Public good characteristics
Distribution system	M^b	M	M	WL, S	Public good characteristics
Terminal system	H	H	H^c	WL, S	Private good, HTC

(Table continues on the following page.)

Table A-1 (continued)

Type of system	Nature of the good		Market power, contestability	Externalities	Comment
	Subtractability	Excludability			
Flood control structures	L	L	L	PH	Public good
Hydropower generation	M	H	H		Private good
Instream uses					
Amenity uses	L	L	M		Public good
Access for fishing and recreation	M	M	M	WP	Can be open access resource
Navigation					
Piers and locks	M	H	H	WP	Toll good characteristics
River channel	L	M	H	WP	Could be toll good or public good

Note: PH, public health; WL, water logging; WP, water pollution; GD, groundwater depletion; ND, introduction of new diseases; SF, difficult to exclude users due to social factors; S, salinization; E, erosion during construction and because of migration into the area; L, low; M, medium; H, high; HTC, high transaction costs for trades beyond the tertiary canal.

a. The degree of subtractability associated with a given well actually depends on the nature of the aquifer from which the well is drawing. High water resource scarcity is assumed.

b. The degree of subtractability depends on the scarcity of water and the capacity of the canal.

c. Function is usually performed by private farmers.

Table A-2. Market Conditions and Public Policy to Assure Efficient Production and Management of Water Resources

Type of good	Provision	Production
Public goods	Full or majority public ownership and public capital financing to ensure adequate allocation of resources.	Where feasible and desirable, rights should be granted to private sector or water user organizations to operate publicly owned facilities under regulation and contract. Otherwise, the public sector should produce the service, such as flood control and large multipurpose dams.
Toll goods	If there are concerns with equitable access to users, market power, scarcity of substitutes, or optimal provision of the good or service, public regulation will be needed regarding property rights, conditions of competition, and quality and pricing of toll services. Since the services are not fully subtractable, a two-part pricing system (one part being a fixed access/connection charge, one part being variable, based on extent of use) is appropriate; but if subtractability is very low, some public financing mechanism (for example, through benefit taxes such as land taxes) might be necessary to supplement direct user charges. Conventional sewerage and navigation are good examples of toll goods.	Should be private, or based on a user organization subject to regulation as noted.
Open access goods	Typically full or majority public ownership with the public being defined to include communities of water users (for example, a community of irrigators).	Mostly private or based on a user organization, but regulation is needed to grant limited property rights (rights to exploit resources or generate services from facilities). Pricing should be based on the scarcity value of the good, but since nonpayers cannot be excluded, indirect financing through a budgetary mechanism may be needed (see the discussion on toll goods). Regulations are also needed if overuse of a resource such as groundwater can destroy its future usefulness (for example, salt water intrusion and aquifer compaction).

(Table continues on the following page.)

Table A-2 (continued)

Type of good	Provision	Production
Market power	Policies and regulations that remove barriers to entry and competition (for example, allow equitable access of potential entrants to capital financing), promote contestability (for example, contract out the operations of water supply systems, the maintenance of irrigation canals, or the collection of water fees), and facilitate availability of substitute services (for example, navigation and hydropower as transportation and energy substitutes, respectively). If minimum investment requirements are very large (economies of scale), some public investment or public capital financing may be needed, which is likely to be the case for large dams and canal systems. For the remaining elements of natural monopoly, regulation of pricing is needed (for example, water companies and electric utilities).	
Externalities	Regulation of investment (for example, land use zoning) and of operations and technical standards (for example, the level of pollutants that a municipal waste treatment plant is allowed to release into a river) are needed. Taxes, fees, or subsidies are imposed to influence private incentives for investment or operation. Regulations are passed that mandate public access to information (for example, the amount of chemicals being released into a lake by industrial firms). The larger the externalities (positive or negative) are, the more justified is public involvement in regulation, provision, and even production (for example, building wastewater treatment plants).	

| Merit goods | Regulation is needed to ensure equitable access to services (such as minimum or universal water services). Investment planning is needed to ensure that some minimum form of service is available. Public financing of investment or current operations is needed for goods whose consumption is considered a social benefit. For other goods, such as wastewater disposal, for which equitable access is considered important, public subsidies of investment or current costs should target groups of users most in need of financial assistance. Pricing policy may be used to differentiate among income groups such as block rates in municipal water supply (may be linked to budget subsidies or cross-revenue subsidies for low-income users). | Mainly private or user organizations, but the public sector may, as a last resort, produce the service if no other source is available. |

Notes

1. This appendix draws heavily on Kessides (1993).

2. Contestability refers to the practical threat of competition from other entrants in a market. In activities with high contestability, entry and exit are relatively costless (for example, the absence of sunk costs incurred in the event of exit).

Appendix B. Water, People, and the Environment: Lessons Learned

This appendix summarizes the lessons learned about the need to integrate concerns about the water environment into economic development policies and actions as part of a comprehensive framework for managing water resources. The lessons generally fit into four categories: improving the quality of surface and groundwater, achieving a cross-sectoral approach, protecting environmental and social values during development, and overcoming concerns about managing water in multiple jurisdictions.

Surface and Groundwater Quality

Placing an emphasis on improving the quality of water is an important element in strategies to reduce poverty. The poor often must use polluted water while many industries gain access to municipally treated water and then return the untreated effluent to waterways. Because they come into contact with polluted water, the poor suffer debilitating diseases. More than 1 billion people are affected by diarrheal diseases each year, and at any one time almost 1 billion people also suffer from roundworm infections, 500 million from trachoma, and 200 million more from schistosomiasis. Moreover, a new generation of colorless and odorless pollutants—toxic pollutants—are discharged by industry and have more serious ramifications for human health, especially for persons who consume tainted finfish and shellfish. Sewage and industrial waste pollute rivers on every continent; estuaries, deltas, and coastal waters are especially affected. With more than 1 billion people suffering from waterborne diseases each year, effective policies to control water pollution are critical elements in a country's strategy for managing water resources.

Another lesson from the industrial world involves implementing pollution control measures so that pollution does not build up downriver to the point where expensive remedial measures are required to treat or remove the deposits. Turning off pollution discharges is not enough when sediment or industrial toxic pollutants have been released, because they are deposited downriver and can interfere with or contaminate aquatic life for decades following cessation of discharges. Repeated dredging of sediment and expensive measures to deal with toxic substances from Germany and the Netherlands to the Great Lakes of the United States and Canada are examples of increased expenditures for remedial actions in the future that were caused by delays in implementing pollution control measures earlier.

As surface water becomes increasingly polluted and costly to purify, water users turn to groundwater as a potential source of a cheaper and safer supply. Groundwater, however, is also becoming polluted by seepage from septic tanks, contaminated soils, disposal of sludges, landfill leachates, unregulated and illegal disposal of hazardous and toxic wastes, and agricultural chemicals. Once contaminated, aquifers are very costly or virtually impossible to clean up. Consequently, emphasis must be placed on preventing pollution and on measures designed to protect aquifers. Land-based pollution prevention programs should target vulnerable geologic areas, recharge areas for important aquifers, and municipal well fields.

For urban water supply, experience indicates that the collection and proper treatment of sewage must be an integral part of water supply projects. Bringing water into a city without taking sewage out exposes the population—and particularly the poor—to increased pollution. Institutions are often not in place to regulate these pollution discharges effectively, nor are the water or fish consumed by the poor in many countries adequately monitored for harmful chemicals. Economic development without strong environmental protection institutions leads to environmental degradation, human suffering, and future costs for remedial actions.

Environmental protection needs to be part of every nation's development strategy. Without a national mandate, arguments over how much pollution control is enough usually dominate the debate. Endless delays occur, and high transaction costs for monitoring, laboratory analyses, and litigation drain funds from government organizations. This was the experience in the United States until national legislation mandated implementation of a minimum level of pollution abatement on all significant sources of pollution. New best practices guidelines for eighty-five pollution sources are being adopted by the Bank and will be published in late 1993. Adoption of such practices will prevent the development of pollution havens, accelerate the cleanup of water resources, and prevent unfair competitive advantages.

A Cross-Sectoral Approach

An important part of the comprehensive framework for water resources management is the integration of concerns about water quality and quantity into traditional sector work involving land use or industrial development. The misuse of land has been fostered by government policies aimed at harvesting forests, farming marginal lands, and draining wetlands for agricultural development. Improper land use has resulted not only in the sedimentation of waterways, in water pollution, and in the destruction of fisheries but also in poverty—as land fails, families are relocated from project areas, and many move to overcrowded cities. Cross-sectoral linkages between land and water management contribute to situations that increase the vulnerability of the poor to disasters, such as crop failures, droughts, landslides, and floods. Prevention and mitigation of vulnerability through the planning of fiscal incentives, the control of land use and land management practices, and sound government policies and programs designed to avoid environmental degradation are less costly and more effective than restoration and recovery costs.

Likewise, cross-sectoral linkages exist between the quantity and quality of water and land-based economic development activities. For example, until the 1960s, the Aral Sea was environmentally stable and had a thriving commercial fishery. The massive diversion of the two largest rivers in Central Asia to expand irrigated cotton production eventually dried up the rivers and shrank the lake by 66 percent. Salinity increased, soils became waterlogged, fish spawning grounds dried up, and the fishery collapsed. Along with these changes, the regional climate changed, thus impairing the growing season for cotton. An ecological catastrophe developed as winds picked up salts and pesticides from the dry lake bed, caused salt and pesticide storms, and ruined the productivity of the farmland.

Excessive withdrawals of water for agriculture have also caused similar, although less extensive, ecological problems in arid areas around the world, including North America. Fisheries have been badly damaged in the formerly productive deltas of the major rivers in India and Bangladesh. Similar diversions for irrigated agriculture in the Tarim

River Basin—China's largest inland river—have dried up the river 230 kilometers from Titema Lake, and the desert has advanced into the area. Lake Chad in Africa provides a similar example. It is clear that, to restore valuable water ecosystems, water must be allocated for ecological purposes in addition to traditional intersectoral purposes.

Desertification refers to the degradation of land-based ecosystems in arid, semiarid, and dry subhumid regions and is mainly the result of adverse human activity. It has recently been declared one of the most serious environmental and economic problems facing the world. Participants at the 1992 Earth Summit in Brazil reviewed a 1991 assessment of the global status of desertification, conducted by United Nations organizations. The assessment found that about 70 percent of all the world's drylands are affected by some form of desertification or land degradation and that areas suffering from desertification had increased 8 percent since the last assessment in the early 1980s. Irrigated agriculture and overgrazing of rangelands were labeled as leading causes, and the direct annual income lost was an estimated $42.3 billion. Annual costs of preventive, corrective, and rehabilitative measures are an estimated $10 billion to $22 billion.

Cross-sectoral issues relating to groundwater in a river basin must also be considered as part of a comprehensive approach to water management. Large cities, such as Bangkok, Manila, and Mexico City, are dangerously depleting their groundwater supplies. Some areas of Bangkok are sinking at a rate of fourteen centimeters each year. Not only does this worsen floods and destroy infrastructure, but the water extraction rates have become unsustainable. In other cases, overpumping of groundwater dries up rivers or nearby village groundwater supplies. In areas where groundwater has been depleted, aggressive demand management and conservation programs should be implemented to help reverse the depletion. Equity considerations for the next generation and prudence in saving confined groundwater for emergencies, such as droughts, dictate that cross-sectoral actions be undertaken to stem depletion of drinking water aquifers, especially if industry or agriculture contributes to the depletion.

These examples of land degradation, declining water quality, ecosystem disturbance, and groundwater depletion have cross-sectoral solutions that should be implemented as part of a comprehensive approach. The world now recognizes that water resources must be managed as valuable natural resources to meet multiple uses. The goal is to accommodate important sectoral uses of water while at the same time sustaining the chemical, physical, and ecological integrity of the water environment. A World Bank paper on the comprehensive approach to water resources management and the environment (Duda and

Munasinghe 1993) outlines lessons learned from including environmental considerations in water resources management.

Social Values and Participation

Single-sector development projects ranging from creating aquaculture ponds in former mangrove swamps to draining wetlands for agricultural conversion or to damming a valley for irrigation or hydropower have had serious and adverse effects on aquatic ecosystems and biodiversity. These development projects can also destroy important cultural resources, displace indigenous peoples, and reduce living standards for relocated citizens. In the past, poor people have sometimes lost access to water whose quality and quantity is adequate to sustain them. Traditional riverine communities and indigenous populations have been forced to resettle and either have become further impoverished or have had to change their life-styles. Access to water and related resources, such as fisheries, is essential for the poor and an important element in alleviating poverty.

The Bank's experience demonstrates that early and full popular participation in planning for river basin management and for specific projects contributes to the design and implementation of successful projects. Participation helps to ensure that environmental resources are protected and that cultural values as well as human rights are respected. Early participation, coupled with identification of the full range of alternative actions for an environmental assessment process, provides guidance for decisionmaking. Significant traditional water structures, including historic gardens and temples, are sacred to local peoples, whose concerns, as voiced during the environmental assessment process, should be recognized. Governments should place special emphasis on meeting the needs of indigenous peoples—that is, governments must ensure that they receive culturally compatible social and economic benefits. Participation can help coordinate interests, increase transparency and accountability in decisionmaking, and encourage user ownership—all of which increase the probability of a project's success.

Managing Water in Multiple Jurisdictions

Implementing comprehensive water resources management within multiple jurisdictions presents a challenge that requires significant international resources to overcome. Development, the reduction of poverty, and the restoration of environmental quality will be enhanced by greater cooperation, trust, and shared authority. For rivers that cross provincial or state boundaries, Colombia, India, Japan, and the United

States, among others, have created multipurpose agencies with broad charters to foster balanced economic development and water management. The Tennessee Valley Authority (TVA) is one such agency, which has helped bring prosperity to a once-poor seven-state section of the southern United States. The TVA has promoted the linkage of land and multipurpose, real-time water management in a comprehensive manner as a way to conserve natural resources. During the 1980s it initiated a dialogue with the business community, NGOs, government officials, and private citizens interested in conducting a regional environmental assessment. The objective was to evaluate alternatives for operating its dams. The result was a new set of operational guidelines and environmental improvement investments that are being implemented to improve water resources management and restore the basin's ecosystem. In conjunction with this new approach, TVA is facilitating interagency cooperation, on a federal, state, and local governmental level, to coordinate management of land and water resources. Through this program, which is operated by an interagency steering committee, water pollution and environmental impacts caused by agricultural, mining, forestry, and urban development are being reduced. The TVA serves as a facilitator to coordinate fragmented interagency actions and encourage local cooperation to improve the coordination of separate land management programs. The objective is to protect the quality of surface and groundwater.

For international waters, similar lessons have been learned that can be used elsewhere to promote joint management of international water resources. Institutional barriers can be overcome through the involvement of all relevant jurisdictions, interagency cooperation, public participation, and data sharing. Independent oversight and advice can be provided by joint commissions composed of members from each nation, such as the long-standing International Joint Commission serving Canada and the United States. Established by treaty in 1909, the commission is an independent, quasi-judicial institution established to (a) provide a process for regulating the level and flow of boundary and transboundary water, (b) develop principles for resolving disputes related to the quantity and quality of waters and for their equitable use, (c) create a framework for fact-finding investigations of water to come to a consensus on needed actions and then provide this advice to the various parties, and (d) involve the public in the decisionmaking process. The commission also oversees implementation of the 1972 Great Lakes Water Quality Agreement, with binational oversight boards and an independent secretariat that evaluates the progress made in cleaning up pollution, facilitates the building of consensus, and provides advice based on their independent evaluation of facts. Remedial measures to improve environmental quality are targeted on problem watersheds, with the commission providing independent reviews of progress that help hold governments accountable for their actions. Water quality has steadily improved during the past twenty years, and transboundary issues such as groundwater contamination and atmospheric transport of toxic substances have recently been addressed.

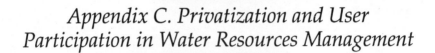

Appendix C. Privatization and User Participation in Water Resources Management

In most developing countries, the development and management of water resources have traditionally been dominated by the central government. It was believed that only the state was able to handle the large investments and operations necessary for irrigation and water supply systems and that the crucial role played by water justified government control. The fiscal crisis in the developing world that began in the early 1980s, however, demonstrated the weakness of much of this argument. The deteriorating irrigation systems and the still-inadequate water supply infrastructures throughout the developing world have exposed the serious institutional deficiencies of many government agencies responsible for water resources. These include lack of motivation and accountability of agency staff, high levels of political interference, and inadequate concern for the needs of users. Consequently, users are not motivated to share in the costs of investments and maintenance or to pay for services.

Solving these problems requires many interrelated reforms. One approach gaining support is to increase the use of the private sector through concessionaire contracts, management contracts, private ownership, and participation by users and communities in managing water resources. This approach can introduce appropriate incentives that provide a sense of responsibility for water systems, improve accountability and concern for users' needs, constrain political interference, increase efficiency, and lower the financial burden on governments.

User and private sector participation in water management is not new. Communal irrigation systems have existed for generations in countries such as India, Indonesia, Nepal, the Philippines, Sri Lanka, and Thailand, while the development of private wells has been a major source of irrigation expansion for the past two decades. But the idea has often been resisted by vested bureaucratic interests or has been rejected due to lack of confidence in the capacity and incentives of the private sector. However, the continued decline in the performance of irrigated agriculture and the inadequacy of water supply systems have brought this top-down approach under greater scrutiny. This appendix reviews the experience of initiatives promoting private sector and community involvement in managing irrigation and water supply. The examples come from Latin America, North Africa, and Southeast Asia, and all demonstrate the clear link between participation or ownership and the improved performance and sustainability of the system.

Irrigation Systems

The hierarchical central control system described in the previous section is remarkably typical in the development and management of large- and medium-scale irrigation projects. In many developing countries, the state has designed and planned irrigation systems according to its needs, without consulting those who use the system. The weakness of this approach has been in maintaining these irrigation systems over the long term. Too often, irrigation agencies have concentrated on developing new systems at the expense of maintaining existing ones. Once built, many agencies are not able to perform the necessary operations and maintenance (O&M). Agencies that levy a water charge to pay for O&M have difficulty collecting it, because farmers are unwilling to pay for poor service. Subsequent government subsidies to pay for O&M are often diverted to pay for new construction.

For these and other reasons, including farmers in irrigation management is seen as a way to stabilize, if not improve, most irrigation systems. One approach has been to increase user participation, which improves the flow of information, establishes a sense of ownership, and gives farmers proper incentives to ensure the system's sustainability. These concepts are lacking in many government-managed systems. Farmers believe, because they had no say in the original design and planning of a state irrigation system, that they are not responsible for maintaining it. Examples show that when the knowledge and experience of farmers are included in planning, developing, and operating an irrigation system, its performance improves. In addition, farmers are more willing to contribute to the upkeep if they have a stake in the system. Another approach is to encourage farmers to develop irrigation privately through commercial systems or individually developed wells. Both communal systems and the development of private wells have contributed significantly to the development of irrigation. The following examples show four different approaches to introducing private sector incentives: (a) forming water user associations,[1] (b) transferring management functions from government authorities to water user associations, (c) introducing irrigation service fees, and (d) developing private wells. Most, but not all, of the examples have some form of Bank assistance. All, however, demonstrate the effectiveness of involving farmers in the management of irrigation.

Water user associations

The following examples demonstrate the effectiveness of water user associations in managing small-scale irrigation systems and tertiary canal networks. These are systems where the associations to either already existed or were newly developed.

ARGENTINA. Traditional irrigation associations in Mendoza covered 100 to 500 hectares but were not large enough to meet the associated costs. Maintenance was insufficient, the administration was weak, and those at the head of the canal benefited the most. The situation changed when the small associations merged into larger ones of between 5,000 and 15,000 hectares. Twenty-one new organizations were formed, covering 200,000 hectares. Each organization is autonomous, raises its own budget, and issues its own regulations in accord with the recently enacted water law. The organization hires professional managers to deal with all administrative matters, such as water delivery, cost recovery, and maintenance. Administrative costs decreased with the decline in the number of associations. The larger organizations have increased the efficiency of conveyance by 10 percent through more efficient distribution. Early results of the shift to larger associations are positive.

NEPAL. Farmer-managed irrigation schemes have a long tradition in Nepal, where 70 percent of all irrigation is controlled by farmers. Nevertheless, the government had been heavily involved in developing new irrigation, with poor results. With a shift in approach, the government now promotes farmer management as a way to improve irrigation performance and to reduce the financial burden on the government of developing and operating irrigation systems.

The Bank responded to the shift in emphasis by financing the Irrigation Line of Credit Pilot Project with resources totaling close to $20 million. The pilot project funds small- and medium-size surface and groundwater schemes that are owned, operated, and maintained by legally recognized water user associations. The association must request the investment, contribute to capital costs, and accept full responsibility for O&M when construction is completed.

The results are impressive. In the first two years of operation, forty-three surface subprojects of the Irrigation Line of Credit were completed out of sixty-one subprojects processed and approved for implementation, and eighty-one tubewells were drilled. Altogether, these subprojects serve an area of some 3,400 hectares and about 4,500 households in eight districts. The project's success is due to the enthusiastic cooperation of farmers and the good dialogue between government officials and farmers. Having water user associations take ownership and responsibility for oversight improved the quality of construction, adding a much-needed element of transparency in the use of government resources. The associations created strong organizations that achieved good cost recovery and levied penalties on members who fail to abide by the rules. Many associations are also involved in other aspects of community development. Overall, the program improved service and reduced costs.

THE PHILIPPINES. About 48 percent of the irrigated area in the Philippines is under the farmer-owned and -managed communal irrigation systems. The government has helped to construct and rehabilitate these systems at least since the 1930s. In the mid-1970s, the National Irrigation Administration (NIA) began a unique participatory system. The process consisted of introducing an irrigation community organizer into a community to encourage farmers to cooperate in O&M. The organizer acts as a catalyst, providing guidance and advice. The farmers participate in all aspects of new development and rehabilitation. A formal, legally recognized water user association is organized to carry on O&M after the NIA withdraws. The procedures governing the association appear complex but work satisfactorily. There is no proof that the agricultural performance of communal irrigation systems improves significantly after these changes, but farmers are very supportive, and O&M costs are met entirely by the beneficiaries.

SRI LANKA. In the early 1980s the U.S. Agency for International Development funded the Gal Oya Water Management Project to rehabilitate the left bank of the Gal Oya River. Following the Philippine model, institutional organizers were introduced into the system. Gaining the trust of the farmers, they began to organize larger groups of farmers along the distribution channels. These groups discussed their problems and communicated with the government irrigation department staff. This process has greatly improved communications between farmers and government officials. Conflict among farmers has declined substantially, and the improved system provides more water for farmers at the tail end of the system. Careful to separate their organizations from party politics, the farmers have also eased ethnic tensions. In one area cooperating farmers cleared a canal allowing 1,000 hectares to be cultivated in the dry season, which had previously been left fallow. This benefited more than 300 families and demonstrated that participation, flexibility, and consensus were the keys to the projects' success.

TUNISIA. Water user associations have existed in Tunisia for most of this century, with the French colonial government introducing their legal basis in 1913. The government of Tunisia reaffirmed the legal status of the associations by legislation enacted in 1975 and in 1987. During the 1970s, however, the government became increasingly involved in developing irrigation. Recognizing the financial burden and inefficiency of this situation, in the mid-1980s the government began to strengthen water user associations and to allow more involvement by the private sector. The Bank supported this change through three irrigation projects and two agricultural sector adjustment loans.

The most success has come in the south, where associations now control practically all tubewell irrigation schemes, ranging in size from 50 to 200 hectares. The farmers are responsible for all O&M, including hiring the appropriate labor and paying for electricity. The associations are well structured technically and financially. While they perform routine repairs, the government performs large repairs, receiving a small contribution from the associations. One notable achievement of involving user associations is that farmers have greater flexibility to respond to changes in market demand for different crops. Previous government control precluded much flexibility.

Transferring control to water user associations

Transferring state-owned and -managed systems to water user associations is more complicated. Farmers may be reluctant to take on what they perceive to be the government's responsibility. Many of the systems need to be rehabilitated before farmers will take them over. Nevertheless, these transfers lower the financial burden on the government and increase the farmers' sense of ownership.

COLOMBIA. Just less than half of the irrigated area in Colombia is managed by the private sector (347,000 hectares); the rest (463,000 hectares) is managed by the Instituto Colombiano de Hidrología, Meteorología y Adecuación de Tierras (Colombian Institute of Hydrology, Meteorology, and Land Improvement), the public sector agency in charge of irrigation and drainage. In 1976 the management of two irrigation districts, the Coello (27,187 hectares) and the Saldaña (13,985 hectares), was transferred to the water user associations, which maintain detailed and comprehensive rules, with elected officials and active participation by the farmers.

A 1989 evaluation by World Bank staff of the Coello district found the system well equipped and managed with sophisticated technology. Operations and maintenance are covered through both fixed and volumetric charges, with the fixed rates covering 50 percent of costs. Fixed and volumetric charges cover nearly 85 percent of expenses, with the remainder coming from equipment rentals, bank interest, and other charges. The success of the system is due to a dynamic farming sector, a high level of farmer training, continuity of staff, simplified operations, and regular maintenance. Rehabilitation work, which began in 1986, was mainly intended to replace obsolete equipment and to introduce modernization.

INDONESIA. No longer able to afford O&M of its extensive irrigation network, the government instituted major policy changes in the irrigation sector beginning in 1987. One policy was to turn over small-scale irrigation systems of fewer than 500 hectares to water user associations. This was supported by the Bank-funded Irrigation Sub-Sector Project (ISSP). The associations were granted formal legal status to enable them to take on management responsibilities. The government carefully prepared the turnover process, bringing farmers in to discuss rehabilitation and redesign and to gain a sense of ownership and responsibility. The International Irrigation Management Institute studied two pilot turnover projects under the ISSP and found that, overall, the maintenance performed was more or less what was required and did not pose a long-term threat to deterioration of the canals. By the middle of 1991 the government had transferred control of more than 400 irrigation systems covering 34,000 hectares to associations. Success for the program relied primarily on including farmers early in the design and construction phase and allowing the formation of associations to be flexible. The program demonstrates the competence of associations in managing irrigation systems.

MEXICO. Three types of irrigation structures exist in Mexico: irrigation units, irrigation districts, and private irrigation. Irrigation units are small-scale schemes that are owned, operated, and maintained by water user associations. Irrigation districts are built, owned, operated, and maintained by the state. These are large-scale schemes of more than 3,000 hectares, containing both large commercial farms and smaller communal farms, or ejidatarios. Because of the continuous budget crisis during the 1980s, the government was unable to keep up with maintenance and other expenditures. Presently, within the state-controlled districts, farmers contribute less than 30 percent of O&M costs through water charges.

Recognizing the need for a new approach, the government, with Bank assistance, is transferring management of the irrigation districts to seventy-eight water user associations. The first stage transfers responsibility for the O&M of the lateral canals and drains. The second stage transfers responsibility of full operations and maintenance for the main irrigation and drainage canals, including water scheduling and distribution. Water charges will be raised to levels necessary to cover the full costs of O&M. The transfer is designed to reduce the government's involvement and expenditures but should also improve the maintenance and sustainability of the schemes. The irrigation districts will become financially self-sufficient and should improve water management. Most important, the project recognizes that the beneficiaries are able to take responsibility for managing irrigation schemes.

THE PHILIPPINES. The NIA has tried to emulate the communal system within the national irrigation system, for which it is solely responsible. After a similar training process, the NIA starts a three-stage process of contracting with the water user associations to perform various levels of O&M and to collect service fees. In the first stage it contracts with the association to carry out O&M under its supervision. In the second stage the association collects irrigation service fees, and incentives are provided to achieve target collection rates. In the final stage responsibility is transferred to the associations for all but the main storage, diversion, and conveyance works. As of 1989, 581 formal contracts covering 140,000 hectares had been signed for O&M of the main system and for the collection of irrigation service fees. Only thirty-five contracts for full transfer had been signed. Overall, results have been favorable, with the majority of associations fulfilling their contracts. The apparent key to the process is the initial introduction of a catalyst to start the process.

Introducing irrigation service fees

Introducing irrigation service fees can be controversial. Often the fees go directly to the central government, which then doles out money according to its own budget. The farmers' incentive to pay the fees relates directly to the service received. If they do not see their money being used to improve the irrigation system, they are unlikely to pay. The following examples illustrate the direct link between willingness to contribute, participation, and service delivery.

INDONESIA. A second policy change was instituted by Indonesia in 1987, the same year the turnover program began. This was the introduction of an irrigation service fee for systems covering more than 500 hectares. This policy depends on the active participation of the users. Pilot projects have shown that the service fee was accepted by the farmers if they were consulted on operations, maintenance, and any rehabilitation or construction works done on the system. When their participation was sought and they felt they had a stake in the irrigation scheme, farmers were more willing to pay the fees.

THE PHILIPPINES. When the NIA gained its autonomy in 1974, its main source of revenue was irrigation service fees. Income from the fees, which have not been raised since 1974, was intended to cover O&M costs. The fees are based on a certain quantity of paddy, so income has been somewhat protected from inflation as long as paddy prices followed the inflation rate. The Administration has had more success in cutting costs than in raising revenues. Although cost recovery has improved, many farmers resist paying the fees because service is poor in many areas and because they oppose paying for an irrigation system over which they have no control. Partly for these reasons, the NIA has embarked on the turnover program described earlier. It is hoped that once farmers have a stake in the system and see service improve, cost recovery will likewise improve.

Developing well irrigation

In many areas groundwater is the major source of water for irrigation. The most extensive use of groundwater resources is probably made in South Asia, particularly in Bangladesh, India, and Pakistan. Here, again, the state was often the initial investor in tubewell development, but was unable to effectively operate and maintain the tubewells, causing them to fall into disrepair and disuse. Farmers invested in tubewells in spite of the state, with greater success.[2] Farmers with the larger holdings and access to capital were the typical buyers of tubewells. However, water markets became common in areas with private tubewells, and poor farmers were willing to pay, often high prices, for water rather than rely on state tubewells. Two examples of private tubewell development come from Bangladesh and Pakistan.

BANGLADESH. Up to the mid-1970s tubewells were developed mostly by the public sector through the Bangladesh Agricultural Development Corporation (BADC). The BADC rented, at heavily subsidized prices, deep tubewells, shallow tubewells, and low-lift pumps. The supply system, however, was limited and inefficient, and the equipment was neglected due to a shortage of parts and qualified maintenance personnel. As the system deteriorated, the Bank encouraged the government to allow private sector investment in the irrigation sector.

Beginning in the late 1970s and early 1980s the government began to eliminate many of the subsidies and import restrictions on agricultural inputs and minor irrigation equipment. This enabled the private sector to compete with the BADC. The sale of pumps for shallow tubewells rose from 4,485 in 1980 to more than 39,000 in 1983. The sale of low-lift pumps rose even more dramatically, from 763 in 1980 to more than 90,000 in 1984. All sales decreased with the reimposition of import and siting restrictions in 1985, but rebounded when the government again loosened all restrictions after the floods in 1988. Between 1988 and 1989 the use of shallow tubewells and low-lift pumps rose 22 percent. By the end of the 1980s the private sector had virtually taken over the market for these two types of equipment.

As in Pakistan, the majority of shallow tubewells are owned by medium to large landholders, although their substantial growth has also benefited small landholders because the market for water has become more active. In one Bank project area, for each owner of a shallow tubewell, there are about fourteen purchasers of water. The Operations Evaluation Department found that for each hectare irrigated by an owner of a shallow tubewell, water purchasers irrigated another two hectares. Bangladesh apparently has ample quantities of groundwater to supply the continuing growth in tubewells, yet the Bank and the government of Bangladesh hope to institute an effective aquifer monitoring system.

PAKISTAN. Public investment in tubewells has a long history in Pakistan. The Salinity Control and Reclamation Project (SCARP), begun in the 1950s, was designed to reduce waterlogging and salinity. Over time, problems of poor maintenance and inefficient installation and management began to emerge. The pumping capacity of SCARP tubewells declined an average of 4–6 percent annually, with 20–45 percent of the tubewells not operating at any one time. SCARP tubewells account for about 10 percent of irrigation water supplies, yet require 55 percent of the total O&M expenditures in the irrigation sector.

The inadequacies of the SCARP tubewells, along with the demonstrated benefits of investments in tubewells, provided incentives for private sector investment. Originally, private involvement came with no encouragement from the government. Slowly, beginning in the 1960s, the government began to liberalize the importation of necessary equipment.

During the following two decades, while continuing to invest in SCARP, the government also encouraged private investment by making credit more available, subsidizing fuel, and extending the electrical grid. Between 1964 and 1976 the use of private tubewells grew about 38 percent annually. By 1990 more than 250,000 private tubewells had been installed, compared with about 13,000 SCARP tubewells.

The performance of private tubewells has been far superior to that of SCARP tubewells. About 90 percent of the private tubewells are operating at any one time, with a shorter downtime because of the growth in small repair shops and the availability of parts. The quality of maintenance is better in private tubewells, most of which are shallow and thus more appropriate for individual farmers. These tubewells increase the farmers' control over the timing and use of supplemental water for irrigation. The development of private tubewells proceeded in spite of public investment and has since replaced public investment at both a savings to the government and a boon to the private sector.

Water Supply Systems

Establishing institutional and regulatory arrangements that foster efficient water supply systems is complicated by the potential for natural monopolies in collecting, purifying, and delivering water. In addition, many households, which are mainly poor, still lack access to decent water supplies, much less appropriate sanitation. In most developing countries, the performance of the water and sanitation organizations is poor, and maintenance is a chronic problem. Many systems are plagued by high levels of unaccounted-for water due to the failure to repair leaks or replace old pipes, the presence of illegal connections, and the lack of meters. In industrial countries unaccounted-for water is about 10 to 15 percent of net production. A recent study by the Bank's Latin American and the Caribbean Technical Department found unaccounted-for water in most Latin American cities ranging from 20 to 50 percent of net production (Yepes 1992:9). The revenue lost as a result of these high water losses are staggering. In Bogotá the revenue losses have been estimated to be equivalent to 25 percent of total billings. "If captured, these financial resources would have been more than adequate to meet all debt service obligations ($195 million) during this period . . . . [In Mexico City the authorities have no] credible plan to meter consumption, maintain meters, and reduce the number of illegal connections. The magnitude of this neglect, coupled with low rates, requires a federal subsidy in excess of $1 billion a year (0.6 percent of gross domestic product), an equivalent to the annual sector investment needed to supply the total population of Mexico with adequate water and sanitation services by the end of this century" (Yepes 1992:v).

Urban water supply

Four types of contracting arrangements are most commonly used in urban water systems: service contracts, management contracts, lease contracts, and concessionaire contracts. With service contracts, a public water company hires a private firm to provide specific services such as reading meters, billing and collecting, and operating production facilities. A management contract lets a contractor assume overall responsibility for operating and maintaining the water supply system, with freedom to make day-to-day management decisions. Under a lease contract a private firm rents the facilities from a public authority and assumes responsibility for O&M. The lessee finances working capital and replacement of capital components with a limited economic life, while the public authority is responsible for fixed assets. With concessionaire contracts, a private firm finances investments in fixed assets, in addition to working capital. Assets are owned by the firm for the period of the concession and are transferred back to the public authority at the end of this period (Yepes 1992:2–3). These arrangements are already observed in several developing countries and are designed to use competitive market forces to improve water management. Three recent examples highlight the Bank's support for privatization in water supply systems.

CHILE. In 1977 the Empresa Metropolitana de Obras Sanitarias (EMOS), the water utility for Santiago, began to encourage its employees to leave the company and form private firms that would bid for service contracts. Contracts were awarded for one to two years under competitive bidding for meter reading, maintenance of the pipe network, billing, vehicle leasing, and more. This approach reduced public employment and costs, shortened response time, and improved service. EMOS is now one of the most efficient public water supply companies in the region, as shown by the number of staff per population served.

CÔTE D'IVOIRE. In the past twenty-five years the urban water sector in the Côte d'Ivoire has been operated by a private company, Société de Distribution d'Eau de Côte d'Ivoire (SODECI), under a mixture of concessions and lease contracts. In 1960 SODECI was established as a subsidiary of a large, French water utility to operate the water supply system of Abidjan under a concession contract. Subsequently, the majority of the equity was acquired by Ivorian shareholders, and shares are traded on the Abidjan stock exchange.

In 1974 SODECI's contract was extended to include three new elements: a lease contract for the O&M of all urban and rural water supply outside the capital, a concession contract for Abidjan including investment in boreholes as well as the O&M of the system, and a maintenance contract for Abidjan's sewerage and drainage. The Water Directorate of the Ministry of Public Works and Transportation was responsible for planning and investment. SODECI collected the approved tariff from consumers, deducted its fees due under the contracts, and transferred the remainder to the two public funds in the water and sanitation sector. Until the arrangements were changed in 1987, SODECI took on limited commercial risk, because it was compensated for any shortfall between actual and projected sales.

For some years this arrangement performed well in important respects. By 1989, 72 percent of the urban population had access to safe water, compared with 30 percent in 1974. About 80 percent of the rural population was served by water points equipped with hand pumps, compared with 10 percent in 1974 (though many of them were not in working order). There was a high level of operating efficiency in urban areas, with unaccounted-for water at 12 percent and the collection rate for private consumers at 98 percent.

These examples demonstrate the potential role for the private sector in providing water supplies. However, a proper regulatory framework must exist for the private sector to be willing to take the risk of investing, even for service contracts. This is perhaps the greatest challenge facing developing countries. The Bank is now trying to help with research and technical assistance to develop these frameworks.

GUINEA. Guinea began to restructure its water supply sector in 1987 and has used leasing contracts to supply water to the principal cities. This has improved the financial conditions of the utility responsible for delivering water and collecting charges, and the efficiency of fee collections has increased from 15 to 70 percent. The process of bidding for lease contracts and the linking of revenues of the lease contractor with cost control and the effectiveness of fee collections creates incentives for efficient operations.

INDONESIA. Indonesia has recently tried a concessionaire contract in East Java. The main component of the project is to build a sixty-five-kilometer transmission pipeline from the Umbulan Springs to Surabaya City. Several groups expressed interest, with the Bromo Consortium, backed by both local and international financing, winning the contract. The concession agreement includes building the pipeline and operating it for a minimum of fifteen years.

Rural water supply

The link between community participation in project development, user responsibility for O&M, and quality of service has been demonstrated by the success of a few rural water supply programs in Africa and South America. Several donors, including the United Nations Development Programme, have been involved in community-managed rural water supply projects. Programs in Colombia and Malawi are examples of community-managed systems with limited government support. Four examples of the Bank's more recent efforts in rural water supply projects are found in Bangladesh, Bolivia, Kenya, and Paraguay.

COLOMBIA. Colombia has the reputation of having the best rural water supply program in Latin America. By 1980, 80 percent of the rural population in Colombia had access to safe water. This is mainly due to a program, developed by the National Institute of Public Health (INS), which encourages community-managed water systems. In each phase of this program, the responsibilities of the INS and the community are clearly spelled out.

The INS provides design standards, instruction materials, and technical assistance for maintenance problems. Also an INS promoter helps the community organize the system's administrative committee and audits the committee's ledgers. With this restricted government support, the contribution of the local community is quite different from mere cost recovery. The community participates in designing the project; elects the administrative committee; raises funds through social activities; and provides materials, labor, transport, and cash for construction. The administrative committee operates, maintains, and regulates the system.

MALAWI. Malawi's program is very similar to that of Colombia. The government's responsibility includes promoting community organization, conducting necessary hydrological and topographic studies, raising external funds, providing engineering designs and standards, assisting in construction, and contributing technical services for maintenance. Also government staff train community leaders in technical and organizational skills. The villagers organize themselves to participate in the project's design and planning, contribute data to pre-project studies, provide labor for constructing the project, and operate and maintain the system.

The result has been quite successful. This program started in a community of 2,000 people and has been replicated throughout the country. Currently, rural water systems owned, maintained, and operated by the community provide 1 million people with safe, reliable, and convenient service. Although ideally suited to small-scale, labor-intensive gravity systems, this program is now being adapted to serve communities reliant on groundwater supplies.

BANGLADESH. In Mirzapur a program of PROWWESS (the Promotion of the Role of Women in Water Supply and Environment Sanitation Services) set out to install hand pumps and latrines. The project was designed to be community based with a strong emphasis on including women. Women were involved from the beginning in selecting sites for hand pumps and latrines. They helped to cure the cement for the platforms and were trained to maintain both the pumps and the latrines. Women were also the main focus of the hygiene education program. In the intervention area, 148 Tara hand pumps (one for every thirty-three inhabitants) and 754 latrines were installed. Most (90 percent) of the households used the hand pump for practically all domestic use compared with only 20 percent outside the intervention area; 98 percent of the adult population said they used the latrines regularly. Within the intervention area, there was a noticeable decline in diarrhea and other diseases. Essential to all of this was the strong participation of women.

The PROWWESS projects recognized that women would not automatically become involved and that a determined effort was necessary to ensure their involvement. The implementing agencies also recognized that male agreement was necessary, and thus the projects did not exclude men. This demonstrates that not only are communities able to manage water supply and sanitation systems effectively on their own, but that women are capable and willing to take the lead in doing so.

BOLIVIA. In a country with the third lowest level of water service and the second lowest level of sanitation service in the western hemisphere, a pilot effort of the United Nations Development Programme and the World Bank has begun to improve water supplies. In 1982 hand pumps were field tested throughout the country, followed in 1988–89 by a program to produce and field test local hand pumps in sixty dispersed rural communities. The program provided technical assistance for the national production of hand pumps based on the design from Bangladesh. Working with PROWWESS and local nongovernmental organizations, the program demonstrated the ability and willingness of small communities to manage and finance their own water supply systems.

Building on this experience, a larger project was proposed in 1990 with financial assistance from the Netherlands. The objectives are to develop a sustainable delivery system providing water supplies and sanitation to 75,000 rural people and to develop an approach that can be replicated in other rural areas. Monitoring and documentation are being conducted to provide a record to use in developing policies and strategies for future programs.

KENYA. In the southern coastal area of Kenya the World Bank teamed up with the United Nations Development Programme and its affiliate agency, PROWWESS, to provide access for the poor to safe water supplies. Beginning in 1983, the project developed and installed hand pumps in rural communities. Early problems prompted the organizers to bring in a local nongovernmental organization specializing in developing self-help water systems and focusing on women's participation. Women were trained as extension workers and in community organizing and development. Both men and women were trained for the appropriate maintenance and repairs. The local nongovernmental organization motivated village men and women to organize themselves into water committees, which would be responsible for maintenance and repairs. By 1988, 135 village water committees existed, all of which had women as treasurers. All of the pumps were functioning. Both men and women had gained greater self-confidence and had an increased respect for, and acceptance of, women in public decisionmaking. In the project area, between 1985 and 1987 diarrhea declined 50 percent and skin diseases 70 percent. The project also resulted in savings for both government and villages.

PARAGUAY. In 1977 the Bank approved the first of two loans for rural water supply and sanitation projects in Paraguay. During the next thirteen years the two projects have served ninety-eight poor rural communities of between 400 to 4,000 people (more than 250,000 total). The first project included household water connections for 50 to 80 percent of the population, with the remainder receiving standpipes, 500 privies, and 2,000 sanitary units (shower, lavatory, and laundry facilities). The second project included 2,000 sanitary units and 2,000 latrines, with 80 percent of the population receiving household water connections. Both projects had basic health education components that were important to their success.

In these rural water supply projects, the communities are responsible for all O&M and pay a portion of the construction costs. To receive support, a community must form a sanitation committee, or junta, and agree to contribute a minimum of 22 percent of investment costs, that is, 10 percent in cash and labor during construction and the remainder as long-term debt (with interest). Tariffs are set according to the socioeconomic level of the community, but nevertheless cover debt payment and O&M, and also contribute to a fund for major repair and replacement of parts.

Despite delays in implementing the projects, mainly due to weaknesses at the government rural water supply agency, the projects have been successful overall. The juntas are motivated, function well, and manage the systems satisfactorily. The tariff structures appear affordable. By 1985 nearly all of the juntas formed for the first project had budget surpluses. Results from the second project show total contributions ranging from 18 to 68 percent (weighted average of 50 percent) of investment costs.

Conclusion

Private sector involvement and user participation in water resource management are not new, but they are still resisted. Unfortunately, water resource agencies tend to impose their will on users, deciding schedules and maintenance as suits their needs. This can result either in inaction on the part of the agency, due to the lack of funds or technical capacity, or in evasion on the part of water users at the expense of equity and efficiency. This inability of most government agencies to satisfy service demands calls for a new approach.

The examples given demonstrate the willingness of the private sector and users to play a larger role in managing water resources and improving water use. User participation and private sector involvement can provide the necessary incentives for stabilizing irrigation and water supply systems and for improving performance. It can add flexibility, transparency, and accountability as well as lessen the financial and administrative burden on the state. For example, a 1989 review by the Bank's Operations Evaluation Department of twenty-one impact evaluations of irrigation projects found cost recovery to be excellent in projects in which management and O&M had been entrusted to water users. Resistance will continue, but greater private sector and user participation offers an effective means to decentralize water resources management and increase the responsibility of users for managing and financing water resource projects.

Notes

1. This paper terms all groups that manage irrigation systems "water user associations." Some countries, however, refer to them as irrigation associations (Philippines) or farmer irrigation associations (Nepal).

2. The major concern with this development of private wells is the possibility of aquifer depletion and local monopoly pricing and the inability of private owners to integrate the management of surface and groundwater.

Appendix D. Summary of World Bank Operational Directives and Other Guidelines Related to Water Resources

OD 4.00—Annex B: Environmental Policy for Dam and Reservoir Projects (April 1989)

This annex sets out the Bank's environmental policies for dam and reservoir projects. The Bank normally only finances projects in compliance with this annex. Governments need to have environmentally and economically sound macroeconomic and sector policies on matters that affect dam and reservoir projects. In the context of individual investment projects, the Bank should review these policies and seek to improve them, if necessary.

Adverse environmental impacts should be avoided, minimized, or compensated for, if possible, during the project's design phase (for example, modification of a dam's location or height) and by measures implemented as part of the project, bearing in mind the need to balance environmental, economic, social, and other concerns. Opportunities to increase benefits should be sought in the design of the project, such as using reservoirs for waterfowl, tourism, and fisheries. Designing water projects in the context of overall plans to develop river basins and regions normally reduces the potential for adverse environmental effects and intersectoral problems that are both unanticipated and cumulative.

During identification, an environmental reconnaissance by independent, recognized experts or by firms—selected by the borrower and approved by the Bank—is essential to (a) ensure that potential environmental effects are identified, (b) ascertain the scope of further environmental studies and actions needed, (c) assess the ability of the borrower to undertake them, and (d) advise on the need for an environmental panel. Information collected is documented and provided to the Bank and to the government agencies concerned to ensure that environmental factors are fully considered in the project's design. These factors include the height and final site of the dam, and they should comprise part of the baseline data against which subsequent changes can be measured.

OD 4.01: Environmental Assessment (October 1991)

This directive provides guidance to staff on the Bank's policies and procedures for conducting environmental assessments of proposed projects. The purpose of the environmental assessment is to improve decisionmaking and to ensure that the project options under consideration are environmentally sound and sustainable. All environmental consequences should be recognized early in the project cycle and taken into account in selecting, citing, planning, and designing the project.

Environmental assessments identify ways of improving projects environmentally by preventing, minimizing, mitigating, or compensating for adverse impacts. These steps eliminate the need for costly remedial measures after the fact. By calling attention to environmental issues early in the project cycle, environmental assessments (a) allow project designers, implementing agencies, and borrower and Bank staff to address environmental issues in a timely and cost-effective fashion; (b) reduce the need for project conditionality because appropriate steps can be incorporated into the project's design and alternatives to the proposed project can be considered; and (c) help avoid costs and delays in implementation due to unanticipated environmental problems. They also provide a formal mechanism for coordinating activities among agencies and for addressing the concerns of affected peoples and nongovernmental organizations.

Specific internal procedures have been adopted for conducting environmental assessments, and guidance has been issued for compliance with Bank policies. (This guidance appears as annexes to this operational directive).

OD 4.02: Environmental Action Plans (July 1992)

This directive outlines Bank policy and procedures relating to the preparation of a country environmental action plan by governments borrowing from the International Development Association and the

International Bank for Reconstruction and Development. An environmental action plan describes the major environmental concerns of a country, identifies the principal causes of problems, and formulates policies and concrete actions to deal with them. For a given country, it provides the essential preparation work for integrating environmental considerations into the overall economic and social development strategy. It is a living document that is expected to contribute to the continuing process by which the government plans and implements environmental management. This process should form an integral part of overall national development policy and decisionmaking.

The Bank's contribution to formal environmental planning varies; however, responsibility for preparing and implementing the environmental action plan, which is the country's plan, rests with the government. Bank policy is to foster preparation and implementation of an appropriate environmental action plan in each country, reflect the findings and strategies of the country's plan in the Bank's work, and promote revision of the plan as often as necessary. In this context, the Bank works with each government to ensure that information from the environmental action plan is included in the Bank's planning and development assistance documents. For the Bank, the environmental action plan is an essential source of base environmental information and analysis for planning assistance that lays out development policy and investment priorities while giving appropriate attention to environmental considerations.

OD 4.15: Poverty Reduction (December 1991)

This directive summarizes Bank procedures and guidelines for operational work on poverty reduction. It incorporates (a) the recommendations included in the policy paper *Assistance Strategies to Reduce Poverty* (1991b), which was based on the guidelines for reducing poverty contained in the *World Development Report 1992* (World Bank 1992d) and endorsed by the Board on 24 January 1991, and (b) the guidelines on poverty work that are covered in other directives and modified, as appropriate, to reflect current policy. The *Poverty Reduction Handbook* (World Bank 1992c), in particular, contains examples of good-practice analytical and operational work and is fully consistent with this directive. The objective of both the directive and the handbook is to strengthen the focus on poverty reduction in the Bank's operations.

OD 4.20: Indigenous Peoples (September 1991)

This directive provides policy guidance to ensure that indigenous peoples benefit from development projects and to avoid or mitigate potentially adverse effects on indigenous peoples caused by Bank-assisted activities. Special action is required if Bank investments affect indigenous peoples, tribes, ethnic minorities, or other groups whose social and economic status restricts their capacity to assert their interests and rights in land and other productive resources and makes them vulnerable to becoming disadvantaged in the development process.

The Bank's policy is that the strategy for addressing the issues pertaining to indigenous peoples must be based on the *informed participation* of the indigenous people themselves. Thus, the core activity of any project that affects indigenous peoples and their rights to natural and economic resources is identifying local preferences through direct consultation, the incorporation of indigenous knowledge into project approaches, and the appropriate, early use of experienced specialists.

For an investment project that affects indigenous peoples, the borrower should prepare a development plan that is consistent with the Bank's policy concerning indigenous peoples. Any project that affects indigenous peoples is expected to include components or provisions that incorporate such a plan.

OD 4.30: Involuntary Resettlement (June 1990)

The objective of the Bank's resettlement policy is to ensure that the population displaced by a project receives benefits from it. Involuntary resettlement is an integral part of project design and should be dealt with from the earliest stages of project preparation, taking into account five policy considerations:

1. Involuntary resettlement should be avoided or minimized, if feasible, exploring all viable alternative project designs.
2. Where displacement is unavoidable, resettlement plans should be developed. All involuntary resettlement should be conceived and executed as *development programs*, with resettlers provided sufficient investment resources and opportunities to *share in the project's benefits*. Displaced persons should be (a) compensated for their losses at full replacement cost prior to the actual move, (b) assisted with the move and supported during the transition period, and (c) assisted in their efforts to improve their former living standards, earning capacity, and level of production, or at least to restore them. Particular attention should be paid to the needs of the poorest groups to be resettled.
3. Community participation in planning and implementing resettlement should be encouraged.
4. Resettlers should be integrated socially and economically into host communities so that any adverse impacts on the host communities are minimized.

5.   Land, housing, infrastructure, and other compensation should be provided to the adversely affected populations, indigenous groups, ethnic minorities, and pastoralists, who may have usufruct or customary rights to the land or other resources taken for the project. The absence of legal title to the land will not be a bar to compensation.

OD 7.50: Projects on International Waterways (April 1990)

Projects on international waterways require special handling, because they may affect relations not only between the Bank and its borrowers but also between countries, whether members of the Bank or not. The Bank recognizes that the cooperation and goodwill of riparians is essential to the most efficient use and exploitation of international waterways for development purposes. The Bank, therefore, attaches the utmost importance to having riparians enter into appropriate agreements or arrangements for the efficient use of the entire waterway system, or any part of it, and stands ready to assist in achieving this end. When differences remain unresolved, the Bank, prior to financing the project, will normally urge the country proposing the project to offer to negotiate in good faith with other riparians to reach appropriate agreements or arrangements. The Bank will not finance projects on international waters that would cause appreciable harm to other riparians.

OD 14.70: Nongovernmental Organizations in Bank-Supported Activities (August 1989)

This directive sets out a framework for involving nongovernmental organizations (NGOs) in activities supported by the Bank. It provides staff with guidance on working with these organizations, bearing in mind their potential contribution to sustainable development and poverty reduction as well as the need to consult with relevant member governments and to proceed in conformity with government policies toward NGOs.

Staff are encouraged, whenever appropriate, to involve NGOs, particularly local ones, in Bank-supported activities, bearing in mind their strengths and weaknesses. However, because of the Bank's relationship with member governments, staff must operate in the framework of the relevant government's policies regarding NGOs. Given the potential benefit to be gained by involving NGOs in development activities, staff should encourage constructive working relationships among governments, donors, and NGOs. The Bank may provide advice to interested governments on approaches and policies for encouraging the development of indigenous NGOs as effective development agents. Successful replication of local initiatives supported by them may be possible only in a political environment that allows NGOs to flourish and multiply.

Staff should be responsive, and encourage governments to be responsive, to NGOs that request information or raise questions about Bank-supported activities, subject to certain restrictions, including preserving the confidentiality of privileged information and the dialogue between the Bank and the government. If NGOs give the Bank information, the extent of confidentiality should be agreed in advance.

Administrative Manual Statement 1.10: Disclosure of Information (June 1989)

This directive states the policy of the Bank on the disclosure of information. Organizational units may, if they consider it necessary, adopt more detailed provisions for information for which they are responsible. The Bank's policy is to be open about its activities and to welcome, and seek out, opportunities to explain its work to the widest audience possible. The presumption is in favor of disclosure, outside and within the Bank, in the absence of a compelling reason not to disclose.

Effective functioning of the Bank, however, does require some derogation from complete openness. Constraints are kept to a minimum. One is confidentiality: information provided to the Bank on the explicit or implicit understanding that there will be no external disclosure, and that access within the Bank will be limited, must be treated in accordance with that understanding. A second constraint arises from the Bank's concern as an employer to respect the personal privacy of its staff: information concerning individual staff members may not be released except in specified circumstances. Third, information should not be disclosed outside the Bank if, because of content, wording, or timing, doing so would be detrimental to the interests of the Bank, a member country, or Bank staff (for example, if doing so would adversely affect the relationship between the Bank and the country because of the frankness of the views expressed or might prejudice the Bank's negotiating position). This does not preclude disclosure of information simply because it is negative. Balanced information, reporting the failures as well as the successes achieved through Bank financing, enhances the perception of the Bank as a technically competent institution that learns from its mistakes.

Some information held by the Bank will not fall clearly into any of these three categories (published, available to specific audiences, or restricted). Whether and to whom such information should be disclosed is a matter of staff judgment, with the indicated presumption being in favor of disclosure.

OMS 2.12: Project Generation and Design—Local Involvement (August 1978)

Involving local executing agencies and intended beneficiaries in a project's design, implementation, and operations may produce a simpler, less costly operation. It may also engender a greater commitment to implement the project components aimed at particular target groups, improve the quality of the project's design, and produce technical, institutional, or managerial solutions. Such success often depends on the care taken in the following:

- Consulting with the intended beneficiaries before defining the project's objectives, major design features, or both
- Investigating the beneficiaries' attitudes toward change, including their willingness to invest labor and capital to achieve the project's purpose
- Identifying possible obstacles that are likely to hinder the intended beneficiaries' access to the project's benefits.

OMS 2.22: Financial Performance Covenants for Revenue-Earning Enterprises (February 1984)

This statement outlines the Bank's approach to the design and use of financial performance covenants as conditions of project lending. It applies not only to private, profit-generating companies but also to revenue-earning public (or mixed) enterprises that are expected to:

- Recover costs by selling their products and services
- Earn a reasonable return on invested capital and make a reasonable contribution to expansion after meeting their operating costs and debt service obligations.

When the immediate achievement of satisfactory financial performance is not practicable, the covenants are a statement of objectives for improving that performance over a reasonable period of years. Because successful performance under these covenants is very much dependent on the commitment of the revenue-earning entity and its government to the objectives, the standards prescribed should be realistic and acceptable to the Bank and other parties involved. If there is substantial doubt about the ability or willingness of the other parties to achieve such standards, it would be preferable not to make the loan.

OMS 3.72: Energy, Water Supply, Sanitation, and Telecommunications (September 1978)

Projects in the energy, water supply and sanitation, and telecommunications sectors serve a variety of purposes, including the provision of basic needs for the urban and rural poor, of amenities highly regarded by all income groups, and of fundamental, capital-intensive infrastructure for economic development.

The Bank has no rigid requirements for the type of organization to which it lends and considers each case on its own merits. However, the Bank always tries to ensure that its borrowers in these sectors have a reasonable measure of autonomy, that they control costs, and that they are financially viable. The main reason behind the Bank's encouragement of a borrower's autonomy are twofold: (a) the customary procedures of government departments are generally not well-suited to the efficient management of public utilities; (b) these borrowers earn revenue and should be reasonably commercially oriented. Given the difficulties that many borrowing countries face in mobilizing public savings, the absence of capital markets, and the competing demands of sectors that do not earn revenue, the Bank requires the borrower's revenue to cover all operating costs and debt service as well as a reasonable part of the investment program, usually varying between 20 and 60 percent.

Vice President's Policy Note: Financing Operations and Maintenance in Irrigation (March 1984)

This policy note reflects the growing concern over the efforts to recover the costs of investment and of operations and maintenance (O&M). A review of irrigation projects found that government efforts to raise revenue for irrigation have been typically weak. This has led to inadequate funding for O&M. This is a problem both of resource mobilization and of allocation, not a problem of cost recovery or of water charges per se. Efficiency and equity goals probably cannot be addressed unless the financial needs of irrigation are met. Long-term objectives should include mobilizing finances by capturing rents from the parties who benefit from irrigation. An important short-term objective of irrigation policy should be to ensure that revenues provided to irrigation authorities are, at least, sufficient to meet the costs of O&M and thus:

- At the project appraisal stage, assurances will be required that sufficient funds are available for O&M.
- At the same time, there has to be adequate recognition that the longer-term objective is to have a system of resource mobilization that will recover capital costs and thus permit investments to be replicated.
- The mobilization of resources should include capturing rents from the parties who benefit directly from irrigation, unless there are specified reasons (for example, equity) why governments choose not to do so.
- In any event, whatever the mode of resource mobilization, an analysis is necessary to determine how the fiscal system affects farmers' incentives.

OPN 2.10: Irrigation Water Charges, Benefit Taxes, and Cost-Recovery Policies (June 1980; superseded by the Vice President's Policy Note of March 1984 on Financing Operations and Maintenance in Irrigation)

As stated in this paper, Bank policies for irrigation water charges and benefit taxes are based on the principles of economic efficiency, income distribution, and public savings. To meet the goal of efficiency, the volumetric pricing of water is desirable in all irrigation projects. If metering is too difficult, it may sometimes be feasible to use alternative charging schemes that have similar efficiency effects. Unless these are constructed carefully, however, they may distort cropping patterns and water use.

Where efficiency pricing is not feasible, it is then necessary to levy a benefit tax, such as a land-improvement tax. This tax should preferably incorporate a degree of progressivity. Also, it may be desirable for the government to collect more revenues than would result solely from efficiency pricing.

There is no prima facie reason why any particular share of costs, such as O&M costs, should normally be recovered. If all, or most, beneficiaries have levels of income below or near the poverty level, then cost recovery may well be close to zero. Also, it may be desirable to include a grace period in the early years of the project, when beneficiaries pay substantially less than at full development.

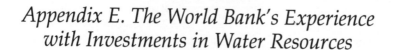

Appendix E. The World Bank's Experience with Investments in Water Resources

This appendix relies on Bank appraisal, completion, and audit reports and on studies conducted by the Operations Evaluation Department (OED). The scope of the review is limited to water projects that were completed and evaluated in the past twenty years and featured irrigation, water supply and sanitation (WSS), hydroelectric generation, and multipurpose projects. The focus is on issues discussed in the text.

Although the review may appear to present a negative view of the Bank's experience, Bank financing has, in fact, made a significant contribution to development. For instance, the Bank helped develop least-cost solutions to infrastructural needs in most of its WSS projects. As a result, potable water was made available to a large population in some of the world's largest—and poorest—cities. Bank investments in irrigation have had a significant role in alleviating poverty and in fostering food security around the world. And Bank financing of hydroelectric generation has produced least-cost supplies of this important addition to the quality of life.

Sectoral and Intersectoral Objectives

Most water projects are implemented by single-purpose agencies, and project goals mirror those of the agencies. The sectoral organization of the Bank adds to this orientation. Moreover, project evaluations are based on the achievement of sectoral objectives. Consequently, concerns for intersectoral allocation of water, downstream effects of water withdrawals, and efficient rationing of water resources are limited.

A review of the few Bank-financed multipurpose water projects demonstrated the value of an intersectoral master plan for water. Three projects stand out as examples of how good planning can lead to positive results: the Sidi Salem Multipurpose Project in Tunisia, the Chungju Multipurpose Project in the Republic of Korea, and the Vasilikos-Pendaskinos Irrigation Project in Cyprus. All of these projects were designed to address problems of acute water scarcity with the intention of maximizing regional development despite a limited supply of water. The success of multipurpose projects depends on creating institutional arrangements for intersectoral coordination. Such arrangements that have proved effective include regional development authorities, interministerial committees, and autonomous enterprises.

Also with intersectoral dimensions, watershed management has been mentioned as a critical factor in the sustainability of irrigation and hydroelectric projects. The Bank has had little experience with watershed management projects. This type of project is atypical of the Bank's efforts to control, store, and transport water to a location where it can be used for socioeconomic development. Although the Bank is increasing its efforts in this field, so far only three projects have been evaluated, and results have been mixed.

There is little discussion of intersectoral use of water in most staff appraisal reports, project completion reports, and project performance audit reports. Many reports attribute water shortages to drought (mostly in Sub-Saharan Africa) and to poor hydrometeorological information (in the Philippines), but rarely to competing uses. Also, efficient management of groundwater resources is usually ignored. The availability of sufficient water for the project's purposes is taken for granted at the appraisal stage and not reviewed afterward. Only when international sources of water are involved has the Bank required a review of water-use rights.

Cost Recovery and Demand Management

The collection of fees for using water is important for irrigation and for WSS projects. Fees can be used both to ensure the financial sustainability of water supply systems and to ration the withdrawal of scarce water. The Bank has maintained the policy that cost recovery should be sufficient to pay both for operations and maintenance (O&M) and for a fair return on capital investment. To ensure that water charges are appropriate, loan covenants have been employed, although they have often been ignored. In fact, in an OED review of completed irrigation projects, cost recovery was rated as unsatisfactory in 80 of 114 projects. And, in 78 percent of the countries receiving WSS loans, financial covenants were not fulfilled. In 49 of the 120 WSS projects, fees were not raised enough to meet financial requirements due to government constraints. Furthermore, the OED report states that, in hindsight, some of the 120 project loans should not have been approved because they were not "bankable" from a financial management perspective.

Even with the increasing cost of supplying water, fee levels that are sufficient to recover costs may not be high enough to ration water use efficiently. Furthermore demand management has not been a priority because many governments are reluctant even to collect sufficient fees for cost recovery. Moreover, although WSS institutions that received Bank loans delivered the bulk of water to middle-class and upper-class residents and industry, water was often subsidized. Fee structures designed for proper demand management have been in place, however, in the successful, Bank-supported WSS systems in Botswana and Singapore.

In irrigation the quality of service provided is linked directly with the ability to collect user fees. Proper maintenance and reliable water delivery are critical for full cost recovery. Thus, Bank reports suggest that irrigation systems be rehabilitated to improve the ability to collect water fees. Indeed, successful collection of fees from irrigation users in a pilot project in Indonesia has been linked to rehabilitation of the system, improved communications, and farmer participation in operations.

Operations and Maintenance

The physical sustainability of both irrigation and WSS projects has been hampered by poor maintenance. In 67 out of 123 completed irrigation projects, O&M was rated as unsatisfactory. Insufficient funding, poor construction standards, and weak planning at the appraisal stage were cited as reasons for the inadequacy. The OED also noted a tendency to support project construction and not O&M. OED reviews of both irrigation and WSS projects have thus highlighted the need for the Bank not to detach itself from postconstruction activities.

The efficiency of water supply systems can be evaluated by measuring unaccounted-for water, which is defined as the amount of water that enters a system less the amount that can be accounted for. Thus, unaccounted-for water assesses the performance of both maintenance and operations by summing the physical loss of water in a distribution system and the administrative loss of billable water. It is the only commonly reported gauge of a system's performance, but it accurately measures efficiency only when the implementing agency is committed to sound administrative controls. Although unaccounted-for water of 25 percent or more is considered problematic, a 1987 Bank review of 54 WSS projects showed an average figure of 34 percent, with a 3 percent annual increase during a six-year project cycle. In the 120 project completion reports and project performance audit reports reviewed by the OED concerning water supply, difficulties related to unaccounted-for water were cited often.

The efficiency of irrigation operations has also been an issue in water policy. But the efficiency of water use in irrigation projects is generally not reported in completion and audit reports. An OED review of impact evaluation studies found, however, that central control and rotation systems, in which delivery was rigidly scheduled by project authorities, resulted in poorly timed and inflexible distribution of water. Correspondingly, systems designed to provide water on demand worked efficiently. For example, the simple gravity system employed in the Sinaloa project in Mexico operated well, although the arranged-demand delivery system required a high degree of training and dedication on the part of project staff.

Farmer participation in water management and in O&M is recommended by all Bank studies on irrigation. Positive results have been demonstrated by Bank projects when water user associations have been introduced. The review of twenty-one impact evaluations found that when responsibility for water management and O&M were given to user groups, the rates of cost recovery were excellent. The impact evaluation of the San Lorenzo project in Peru found that the irrigation systems were fully operated and maintained by self-supporting water user associations. Through the Irrigation Subsector Projects in Indonesia, the Bank is supporting the government's effort to give user groups responsibility for managing and controlling irrigation systems smaller than 150 hectares. Recent studies of pilot turnover projects show good performance on maintenance.

Similarly, private sector incentives may improve maintenance. In Pakistan, the O&M of the Salinity Control and Reclamation Project (SCARP), a publicly financed groundwater development program, has been deteriorating. Pumping capacity has declined an average of 4 to 6 percent annually. SCARP tubewells account for about 10 percent of irrigation water supplies, yet require 55 percent of the total O&M expenditures in the irrigation sector. Between 20 and 45 percent of public tubewells are not operating at any one time. By contrast, 90 percent of private tubewells are operational. Supplies are available in private repair shops, thus shortening the time required for maintenance and repair. Between 1964 and 1976 the number of private tubewells grew 38 percent annually. The Bank has supported this policy most recently through the

SCARP transition projects, which aim to transfer public tubewells to the private sector.

Institution Building, Decentralization, and Privatization

The Bank has placed a great deal of emphasis on developing institutions. Despite these efforts, O&M, financial management, and planning have often been unsatisfactory. Lack of administrative capacity, poor institutional arrangements, and political interference contribute to this poor performance. Furthermore, too many agencies have overlapping responsibilities, and interagency coordination is limited. In an OED review of 120 Bank WSS projects, management organization was often mentioned as a problem. Governmental interference was linked to inappropriate senior appointments, overstaffing, and rapid turnover of staff.

One frequent recommendation made in the irrigation sector is that services be decentralized to the provincial and local levels. But decentralized operations can only be successful if finances are also decentralized. Before the recent irrigation subsector project in Indonesia, farmers complained of having to pay water charges without seeing the funds used in their districts. Government control of cost recovery and O&M has often led to poor service.

In contrast, the National Irrigation Administration in the Philippines is primarily a self-supporting irrigation agency. It raises its own funds to cover O&M of the system, although it receives outside help for new investment. This has forced it to act more like a corporation than a government agency, shedding staff and providing incentives for cost recovery. Service has essentially stabilized, in spite of some complaints. In addition the most recent Bank project in Mexico supports the devolution of responsibility for irrigation operations to the district level by placing irrigation districts in the hands of the farmers, who maintain responsibility for O&M and cost recovery.

Private investment in irrigation is an extension of the push for user participation. Privatization, however, requires an appropriate environment. The most impressive results from privatization come from Bangladesh and Pakistan. In Bangladesh, the Bank encouraged government withdrawal through a series of import program credits in the 1980s. After some initial hesitancy and setbacks, the government has increasingly withdrawn from the sale of shallow tubewells and low-lift pumps. Since allowing private involvement, sales of shallow tubewells and low-lift pumps have grown from about 14,000 in 1983 to more than 49,000 in 1989. Two recent Bank-funded projects—the Shallow Tubewell/Low-Lift Pump Project and the National Minor Irrigation Development Project—both continue this process.

Environmental Issues

Bank appraisal and evaluation documents have, in general, not dealt with water quality. Since most completed Bank projects were designed and implemented before the recent operational directives on the environment (see appendix D), most project reports have little or no discussion of how the project affects the environment. Even when environmental issues are discussed, pertinent issues of water quality, reduced stream flows, and groundwater management are seldom mentioned.

A review of seventeen hydroelectric projects audited by the Bank since 1980 revealed a recent, growing concern for certain environmental issues, especially waterborne health problems, watershed management, and induced seismicity. This review complemented a 1990 study of fifty-nine hydroelectric projects that found a growing concern for environmental effects during appraisal. The number of staff appraisal reports that reported reservoir size increased from 34 percent during 1978–82 to 86 percent during 1988–89. Similarly, during 1978–82, an environmental assessment was undertaken before appraisal in only 31 percent of these projects; during 1988–89, this share increased to 86 percent.

Although more recent Bank projects indicate increased environmental awareness, many concerns, such as water quality, the type of land inundated, the removal of biomass from reservoir areas, the protection of endangered species, and the mitigation of environmental damage, have been given little attention in project reports. Instream uses of rivers were generally ignored. The timing of OED audit studies does not allow for a complete evaluation of environmental effects after the project has been implemented. No impact evaluation has been performed on large-scale dam projects.

Water projects, including Bank-supported projects, have placed a priority on delivering water to urban and agricultural users and given less attention to the corresponding drainage and sewerage systems. The result has been an environmental imbalance of critical importance. A major reason for the neglect of drainage and sewage removal has been that planned systems have not been completely implemented. Although these removal systems have been included in project plans, they are easily ignored when funding becomes scarce.

Half of the twenty-one projects evaluated and featured in a 1989 OED review of irrigation had serious problems of waterlogging and salinity. Drainage networks were often planned but never completed. In one project 17 percent of the area was no longer cultivable because of poor drainage, while in another the figure was 20 percent. In contrast, no such problems existed where the drainage networks were complete. Too often drainage is believed to be an issue that can be handled later. The OED recommends, however, that plans for drainage be made at the same time as irrigation plans.

The production of wastewater is directly proportional to the water supply. Although the Bank has focused its efforts on water supply projects, scant attention has been placed on removing and treating sewage. Despite years of concern for the environmental and health effects of projects, only a few urban areas that were the site of a Bank-funded water supply project have sewer or sanitation systems that are adequate to remove the excess waste generated.

Social Issues

In recent years the Bank has increased its focus on issues such as poverty alleviation, resettlement, and women's roles in development. In the past, however, these issues were often ignored in project reports. For instance the OED review of the WSS sector revealed that projects implemented before 1976 did not address poverty directly, while those appraised since 1981 raised a realistic concern for poverty relief. As previously mentioned, Bank projects did increase the standard of living. For instance, in twenty of twenty-one irrigation projects analyzed in impact evaluations, incomes grew and the standard of living improved. Certainly, some of this increased wealth aids the poor. But the OED has recommended that poverty relief be incorporated into the initial design of a project.

Resettlement of populations displaced by large dam projects is a sensitive issue. The Bank was the first multilateral provider of development assistance to adopt, as early as 1980, a firm policy on involuntary resettlement. Lessons learned from projects in the early 1980s were incorporated into OD 4.30, "Involuntary Resettlement," issued in 1990. All projects entailing involuntary displacement are required to have resettlement plans at the time of appraisal. Requirements for environmental analysis help to ensure that the planning for resettlement begins early. Plans should minimize resettlement. For those who must be resettled, time-bound and specific plans must show how prior standards of living and incomes are to be restored fully or improved. The Bank is working with its borrowers to help develop national policies and legal frameworks for adequate resettlement.

Overall Project Performance Ratings

Although the OED assigns overall performance ratings to most Bank projects, the previous discussion ignored these figures in order to focus

Table E-1. Overall Performance of Evaluated Projects in Selected Sectors for Various Years, 1974–91

Year	Agriculture and rural development		Irrigation and drainage		Water supply and sanitation		Total Bank lending	
	Number evaluated	Percent satisfactory	Number evaluated	Percent satisfactory	Number evaluated	Percent satisfactory	Number evaluated	Percent satisfactory
1974–91	880	65	192	69	153	80	2,863	76
1989	82	56	24	46	10	70	257	70
1990	114	52	28	43	16	56	359	64
1991	94	53	17	71	16	56	276	60
1974–88	590	70	123	80	111	88	1,971	81
1987	66	61	18	78	14	71	185	72
1988	62	60	18	61	15	87	161	74

on issues of water resource policy. This rating system, which reduces project evaluations to a "satisfactory" or "unsatisfactory" rating, is used exclusively in the OED's annual reviews to provide a set of summary indicators. Originally based on the single criterion of whether the estimated economic rate of return exceeded 10 percent, the ratings are now based on a more complete and realistic assessment of operational performance and agricultural production, which takes into account institutional and policy objectives and the projected sustainability of project benefits (table E-1). This may partly explain the recently reported decline in the performance of water projects.

Conclusions

Many issues, such as poor O&M, insufficient cost recovery, and the lack of drainage systems, have long been recognized as problematic. Despite concern, these problems are often repeated. However, the Bank has recently addressed social and environmental issues more explicitly, and these concerns are reflected in project reports.

Based on lessons learned from Bank experience, recent OED reviews of irrigation and WSS projects have included the following recommendations:

- Project planners should carefully assess water resources within a comprehensive framework before the design and implementation stages.
- More detailed guidelines, training, and information should be provided to borrowers, especially for coordinating intersectoral water

resources management, designing and administering fee structures, and monitoring project performance.

- The Bank should consider lending for water services if minimum conditions are met for a healthy expansion of capacity, including autonomy and accountability of management in operations, acceptable levels of unaccounted-for water, and cost-based prices for all except low-income residential consumers.
- Water agencies need to establish and follow arrangements for coordinating their activities. When they must withdraw needed technical services, this should be done gradually and with careful attention to transferring responsibilities to other government agencies, water user associations, or private firms.
- The Bank should not attempt to use cost-benefit analysis to justify projects that fail to consider the environmental damage caused by borrowers' policies.
- Poverty relief should be a project goal at the design stage.
- Adequate data bases should be put in place when the project is being prepared and appraised to monitor and evaluate the impact of Bank lending on the physical environment and on the populations affected by the project.
- Bank staff should analyze O&M capacities and not make major new investments until this capacity has been brought to adequate levels.
- The Bank should help develop WSS organizations that rely less on government involvement in implementation and more on a clear regulatory framework.
- Water users should be given more responsibilities for managing water. In addition, where feasible, emphasis should be given to private pumping and small-scale systems managed by users.
- To protect the environment, drainage networks should be an integral part of the basic design of all irrigation systems, the water table should be continuously monitored for operating irrigation projects, and erosion control and reforestation programs should be an integral part of the project design for reservoir catchment areas.
- For irrigation projects, better construction standards should be promoted through the careful review of the final design and bidding documents, a better selection of contractors, and better supervision of construction. A portion of the loans should be allocated to postcompletion activities such as monitoring.

Bibliography

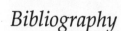

The word "processed" describes informally reproduced works that may not be commonly available through library systems.

Andersen, R. A., and W. R. Rangeley. 1991. "Prospects for Collaboration in the Development of the Many International Rivers of Sub-Saharan Africa." International Water Resources Congress, Rabat, Morocco. Processed.

Anil, Agarwal, James Kimondo, Gloria Moreno, and Jon Tinker. 1981. *Water, Sanitation, Health—For All? Prospects for the International Drinking Water Supply and Sanitation Decade, 1981–90.* London.: Earthscan.

Ansari, Nasiruddin. 1989. "Rehabilitation of Communal Irrigation Schemes in Nepal." ODI Irrigation Management Network Paper 89/1c. Overseas Development Institute, London. Processed.

Aziz, K. M. A., and others. 1990. "Water Supply, Sanitation, and Hygiene Education: Report of a Health Impact Study in Mirzapur, Bangladesh." UNDP/World Bank Water and Sanitation Program. Washington, D.C. Processed.

Berkoff, D. J. W. 1990. *Irrigation Management on the Indo-Gangetic Plain.* World Bank Technical Paper 129. Washington, D.C.

Bhatia, Ramesh, and Rita Cessti. 1992. "Water Conservation and Pollution Control in Industries." Paper presented at a water policy seminar, World Bank, Agriculture and Rural Development Department, Washington, D.C. Processed.

Bhatia, Ramesh, Rita Cestti, and James Winpenny. 1992. "Policies for Water Conservation and Reallocation 'Good Practices' Cases in Improving Efficiency and Equity." World Bank–ODI Joint Study, Infrastructure and Urban Development Department, Washington, D.C. Processed.

Bhatia, Ramesh, and Malin Falkenmark. 1992. "Water Resources Policies and the Urban Poor: Innovative Approaches and Policy Imperatives." Background paper for International Conference on Water and the Environment: Development Issues for the 21st Century, Dublin, Ireland. World Meteorological Organization, New York. Processed.

Bhatnagar, Bhuvan, and Aubrey C. Williams, eds. 1992. *Participatory Development and the World Bank: Potential Directions for Change.* World Bank Discussion Paper 183. Washington, D.C.

Briscoe, John, and David de Ferranti. 1988. *Water for Rural Communities: Helping People Help Themselves.* Washington, D.C.: World Bank.

Bruns, Bryan, and S. D. Atmanto. 1992. "How to Turn Over Irrigation Systems to Farmers? Questions and Decisions in Indonesia." ODI Irrigation Management Network Paper 10. Overseas Development Institute, London. Processed.

Butcher, David A. 1990. "A Review of the Treatment of Environmental Aspects of Bank Energy Projects." Energy Series Paper 24. World Bank, Industry and Energy Department, Washington, D.C. Processed.

Cernea, Michael M. 1988. *Involuntary Resettlement in Developing Projects: Policy Guidelines in World Bank–Financed Projects.* World Bank Technical Paper 80. Washington, D.C.

———. 1992. *The Building Blocks of Participation, Testing Bottom-up Planning.* World Bank Discussion Paper 166. Washington, D.C.

Duda, Alfred M., and Mohan Munasinghe. 1993. "Environment Considerations in Implementing the Comprehensive Approach to Water Management." Environment Working Paper 60. World Bank, Environment Department, Washington, D.C. Processed.

Easter, K. William, ed. 1986. *Irrigation Investment, Technology, and Management Strategies for Development.* Studies in Water Policy and Management 9. Boulder, Colo.: Westview Press.

Easter, K. William, J. A. Dixon, and M. M. Hufschmidt, eds. 1991. *Watershed Resources Management Studies from Asia and the Pacific.* Singapore: Institute of Southeast Asian Studies.

Easter, K. William, and Yacu Tsur. 1992. "Water Shadow Values and Institutional Arrangements for Allocating Water among Competing Sectors." University of Minnesota, Department of Agricultural and Applied Economics, St. Paul. Processed.

Edwards, D. B., Edward Salt, and Fred Rosensweig. 1992. *Making Choices for Sectoral Organization in Water and Sanitation.* WASH Technical Report 74. Washington, D.C.: USAID.

Frederiksen, Harald. 1992a. "Discussion of Some Misconceptions about Water Use Efficiency and Effectiveness." World Bank, Asia Technical Department, Washington, D.C. Processed.

———. 1992b. *Drought Planning and Water Efficiency Implications in Water Resources Management.* World Bank Technical Paper 185. Washington, D.C.

———. 1992c. *Water Resources Institutions: Some Principles and Practices.* World Bank Technical Paper 191. Washington, D.C.

Gerards, Jan L., Birong S. Tambunan, and Bachtiar Harun. 1991. "Experience with Introduction of Irrigation Service Fees in Indonesia." Paper prepared for the 8th Afro-Asian region conference, International Commission on Irrigation and Drainage, Bangkok. Processed.

Gibbons, Diana C. 1986. *The Economic Value of Water.* Washington, D.C.: Resources for the Future.

Gore, Albert. 1992. *The Earth in the Balance.* Boston, Mass.: Houghton Mifflin.

Hearne, Robert. 1992. "A Review of Water Allocation Institutions." World Bank, Agriculture and Rural Development Department, Washington, D.C. Processed.

Hearne, Robert, Charles Sheerin, and K. W. Easter. 1992. "A Review of the World Bank's Experience with Water Resources Investments." World Bank, Agriculture and Rural Development Department, Washington, D.C. Processed.

Jeffcoate, Philip, and Arumukham Saravanapavan. 1987. *The Reduction and Control of Unaccounted-for Water: Working Guidelines*. World Bank Technical Paper 72. Washington D.C.

Kessides, Christine. 1993. *Institutional Options for the Provision of Infrastructure*. World Bank Discussion Paper 112. Washington, D.C.

Kirmani, Syed, and Robert Rangeley. 1992. "International Inland Waters: Concepts for a More Proactive Role for the World Bank." World Bank, Agriculture and Natural Resources Department, Washington, D.C. Processed.

Korton, F. F., and R. Y. Siy. 1989. *Transforming a Bureaucracy: The Experience of the Philippine National Irrigation Administration*. Manila, Philippines: Ateneo de Manila University Press.

Kurup, K. Balachandra. 1991. "Participatory Strategies in Water, Health, and Rural Development Programmes." *Waterlines* 10 (2): 2–5.

Lee, T. R. 1990. *Water Resources Management in Latin America and the Caribbean*. Boulder, Colo.: Westview Press.

Le Moigne, Guy, Shawki Barghouti, Gershon Feder, and Lisa Garbus, eds. 1992. *Country Experiences with Water Resources Management: Economic, Technical, and Environmental Issues*. World Bank Technical Paper 175. Washington, D.C.

Le Moigne, Guy, Robert Rangeley, T. W. Mermel, and Scott Guggenheim. 1991. "Dam Planning, People, and the Environment: World Bank Policies and Practices." World Bank, Agriculture and Rural Development Department, Washington, D.C. Processed.

Livingston, M. L. 1992. "Designing Water Institutions: Market Failure and Institutional Response." World Bank, Agriculture and Rural Development Department, Washington, D.C. Processed.

McPherson, H. J., and M. G. McGarry. 1987. "User Participation and Implementation Strategies in Water and Sanitation Projects." *Water Resources Development* 3 (1): 23–30.

Melchior-Tellier, Siri. 1991. "Women, Water, and Sanitation." *Water International* 16 (3): 161–68.

Morton, James. 1989. "Tubewell Irrigation in Bangladesh." ODI Irrigation Management Network Paper 89/2d. London. Processed.

Munasinghe, Mohan. 1992. *Water Supply and Environmental Management*. Boulder, Colo.: Westview Press.

Muñoz, Jorge. 1992. "Rural Land Markets in Latin America: Evidence from Four Case Studies (Bolivia, Chile, Honduras, and Paraguay)." World Bank, Agriculture and Rural Development Department, Washington, D.C. Processed.

Narayan-Parker, Deepa. 1988. "People, Pumps, and Agencies: The South Coast Hand Pump Project." PROWWESS/UNDP Technical Series. UNDP, New York. Processed.

———. 1989. "Indonesia: Evaluating Community Management; A Case Study." PROWWESS/UNDP Technical Series. UNDP, New York. Processed.

Okun, D. A., and Donald T. Lauria. 1991. *Capacity Building for Water Resources Management*. New York: UNDP.

Patil, R. K. 1987. "Economics of Farmer Participation in Irrigation Management." ODI Irrigation Management Network Paper 87/2d. Overseas Development Institute, London. Processed.

Plusquellec, Hervé. 1989. "Two Irrigation Systems in Colombia." Working Paper Series 264. World Bank, Agriculture and Rural Development Department, Washington, D.C. Processed.

Postel, Sandra. 1993. "Plug the Leak, Save the City." *International Wildlife* 23 (1): 38–41.

Priscoli, J. D. 1992. "Collaboration, Participation, and Alternative Dispute Resolution (ADR): Process Concepts for the Bank's Role in Water Resources." World Bank, Agriculture and Rural Development Department, Washington, D.C. Processed.

Repetto, Robert. 1986. *Skimming the Water: Rent Seeking and the Performance of Public Irrigation Systems*. Research Report 4. Washington, D.C.: World Resources Institute.

Rogers, Peter. 1992a. "Comprehensive Water Resource Management: A Concept Paper." Working Paper Series 879. World Bank, Infrastructure and Urban Development Department, Washington, D.C. Processed.

————. 1992b. "A Note on the Economic Benefits of Cooperation on International River Development." World Bank, Agriculture and Rural Development Department, Washington, D.C. Processed.

Saunders, Robert, Jeremy Warford, and P. Mann. 1977. *Alternative Concepts of Marginal Cost for Public Utility Pricing*. World Bank Staff Working Paper 259. Washington, D.C.: World Bank.

Scheierling, Susanne. 1992. "Agricultural Water Pollution: The Challenge of Integrating Agricultural and Environmental Policies: Lessons from the European Community Experience." World Bank, Asia Technical Department, Washington, D.C. Processed.

Small, Leslie E. 1987. "Irrigation Service Fees in Asia." ODI Irrigation Management Network Paper 87/1c. Overseas Development Institute, London. Processed.

Small, Leslie E., and Ian Carruthers. 1991. *Farmer-Financed Irrigation: The Economics of Reform*. Cambridge: Cambridge University Press.

Smout, Ian. 1990. "Farmer Participation in Planning, Implementation, and Operation of Small-Scale Irrigation Projects." ODI Irrigation Management Network Paper 90/2b. Overseas Development Institute, London. Processed.

Svendsen, Mark. 1991a. "The Impact of Irrigation Financial Self-Reliance on Irrigation System Performance in the Philippines." International Food Policy Research Institute, Washington, D.C. Processed.

————. 1991b. "Recovery of Irrigation Costs through Water Charges." Paper prepared for workshop on irrigation water charges (Khartoum, Sudan), International Food Policy Research Institute, Washington, D.C. Processed.

Svendsen, Mark, and L. Changming. 1990. "Innovations in Irrigation Management and Development in Hunan Province." *Irrigation and Drainage Systems* 4: 195–214.

Terrink, John. 1992. "Water Allocation Methods and Water Rights in the Western States, U.S.A." World Bank, Asia Technical Department, Washington, D.C. Processed.

Triche, Thelma A. 1990. "Private Participation in the Delivery of Guinea's Water Supply Services." World Bank, Infrastructure and Urban Development Department, Washington, D.C.. Processed.

Tsur, Yacov. 1992. "Water Shadow Values and the Allocation of Water among Multiple Uses." World Bank, Agriculture and Rural Development Department, Washington, D.C. Processed.

United Nations Conference on Environment and Development. 1992. "Protection of the Quality and Supply of Freshwater Resources." *Agenda 21.* Vol. 2, chap. 18. New York, N.Y.

UNDP (United Nations Development Programme). 1990. *Safe Water 2000.* New York.

UNDP/World Bank. 1992a. "Improving Services for the Poor: A Program Strategy for the 1990s." World Bank, Transportation, Water, and Urban Development Department, Washington, D.C. Processed.

———. 1992. "Water and Sanitation Program Annual Report 1990–91." World Bank, Transportation, Water, and Urban Development Department, Washington, D.C.

Uphoff, Norman. 1986. *Improving International Irrigation Management with Farmer Participation: Getting the Process Right.* Boulder, Colo.: Westview Press.

Uphoff, Norman, M. L. Wickramasinghe, and C. M. Wijayaratna. 1990. "'Optimum' Participation in Irrigation Management: Issues and Evidence from Sri Lanka." *Human Organization* 49 (1): 26–40.

Vermillion, D. L. 1990a. "Issues Concerning the Small-Scale Irrigation Turnover Program in Indonesia: 1987 to October 1990." Briefing paper. International Irrigation Management Institute, Colombo, Sri Lanka. Processed.

———. 1990b. "Potential Farmer Contributions to the Design Process: Indications from Indonesia." *Irrigation and Drainage Systems* 4: 133–50.

Whittington, Dale, Donald T. Lauria, Albert M. Wright, Kyeongue Choe, Jeffrey Hughes, and Venkateswarlu Swarna. 1992. "Household Demand for Improved Sanitation Services: A Case Study of Kumasi, Ghana." UNDP–World Bank, Water and Sanitation Program. World Bank, Transportation, Water, and Urban Development Department, Washington, D.C. Processed.

World Bank. 1990a. *Annual Review of Evaluation Results, 1988.* Report 8645. Washington, D.C.

———. 1990b. *Annual Review of Evaluation Results, 1989.* Report 8970. Washington, D.C.

———. 1991a. *Annual Review of Evaluation Results, 1990.* Report 9870. Washington, D.C.

———. 1991b. *Assistance Strategies to Reduce Poverty.* A World Bank Policy Paper. Washington, D.C.

———. 1991c. *Forestry: The World Bank's Experience.* Washington, D.C.

———. 1991d. "UNDP–World Bank Water and Sanitation Program, Annual Report 1990–91." Washington, D.C. Processed.

———. 1991e. "UNDP–World Bank Water and Sanitation Program, Work Program. Volume I: Country Work Plan 1991–92." Washington, D.C. Processed.

———. 1992a. "Asia Water Resources Study. Volume I: Main Report." Asia Technical Department, Washington, D.C. Processed.

————. 1992b. "Asia Water Resources Study. Volume II: Annexes 1 and 2." Asia Technical Department, Washington, D.C. Processed.

————. 1992c. *Poverty Reduction Handbook.* Washington, D.C.

————. 1992d. *World Development Report 1992: Development and the Environment.* New York, N.Y.: Oxford University Press.

————. 1993a. *Evaluation Results for 1991.* Report 12400. Washington, D.C.

————. 1993b. "Water Supply and Sanitation Projects: The Bank's Experience, 1967–1989." Operations Evaluation Department, Washington, D.C. Processed.

World Bank Water Demand Research Team. 1993. "The Demand for Water in Rural Areas: Determinants and Policy Implications." *Research Observer* 8 (1): 47–70.

World Meteorological Organization. 1992. "Report to the World Bank on Hydrological Data for Water Resources Management." New York. Processed.

World Meteorological Organization/Unesco (United Nations Educational, Scientific, and Cultural Organization). 1991. *Report on Water Resources Assessment: Progress in the Implementation of the Mar del Plata Action Plan and a Strategy for the 1990s.* New York, N.Y.

Xie, Mei. 1991. "Watershed Management: Main Issues." World Bank, Agriculture and Rural Development Department, Washington, D.C. Processed.

————. 1992a. "Investment Projections in Major Water Sectors." World Bank, Agriculture and Rural Development Department, Washington, D.C. Processed.

————. 1992b. "Wetlands Management: Main Issues." World Bank, Agriculture and Rural Development Department, Washington, D.C. Processed.

Xie, Mei, Ulrich Kuffner, and Guy Le Moigne. 1993. *Using Water Efficiently: Technological Options.* World Bank Technical Paper 205. Washington, D.C.

Yepes, Guillermo. 1992. "Infrastructure Maintenance in LAC: The Costs of Neglect and Options for Improvement." Latin America and the Caribbean Technical Department Report 17. World Bank, Washington, D.C. Processed.